Hawthorne's Prophets

Fay Ellwood's *Hawthorne's Prophets* presents an insightful and authoritative study of the role played by the biblical prophets in Hawthorne's efforts to establish a distinctively American literary and mythological tradition during the early nineteenth century. Her work demonstrates that Hawthorne's understanding of the privileged knowledge of the prophets and their capacity to announce the outworking of the divine will in human life is integral to his own writings.

—Marvin A. Sweeney,
Claremont School of Theology

Hawthorne's Prophets reminds us why early American literature cannot be properly understood without understanding what early Americans would have called the Old Testament. Writing with rare delicacy and singular insight, Fay Ellwood employs a deep knowledge of both literature and scripture to make a compelling argument about American foundational narratives.

—Lori Anne Ferrell, author of
The Bible and the People

MERCER UNIVERSITY PRESS

Endowed by

TOM WATSON BROWN
and
THE WATSON-BROWN FOUNDATION, INC.

HAWTHORNE'S PROPHETS

The Bible and the Creation of American Literature

Fay Elanor Ellwood

MERCER UNIVERSITY PRESS
Macon, Georgia

MUP/ P702

© 2024 by Mercer University Press
Published by Mercer University Press
1501 Mercer University Drive
Macon, Georgia 31207

28 27 26 25 24   5 4 3 2 1

Books published by Mercer University Press are printed on acid-free
paper that meets the requirements of the American National
Standard for Information Sciences—Permanence of Paper for
Printed Library Materials.

Printed and bound in the United States.

This book is set in Caslon

Cover/jacket design by Burt&Burt.

ISBN   978-0-88146-950-9

Cataloging-in-Publication Data is available from the Library of Congress

For Robert and Gracia Fay Ellwood

"Don't adventures ever have an end?
I suppose not.
Someone else always has to carry on the story."
—J. R. R. Tolkien

CONTENTS

Acknowledgments

I would like to thank my father and mother, Robert and Gracia Fay, for teaching me how to be a student, and my brother Richard for keeping my computers running. I thank my peers in the Claremont Graduate University English and Hebrew Bible departments, especially my writing partner, Tara Prescott. I am also grateful to my teachers over the years who made me want to do what they do: Jim Moran, Lyssa Axeen, Jeff Myers, Laurie Kaplan, Martin Griffin, Marc Redfield, Philip Clayton, and Cora Alley. I am also grateful for Mary Marchand who made me fall in love with American Literature, and Kristin de Troyer, my very first Hebrew Bible professor.

I owe a great deal to my doctoral committee: Marvin Sweeney, Lori Anne Ferrell, and Robert Hudspeth. Marvin Sweeney taught me to explore the Hebrew Bible with sensitivity and integrity. Lori Anne Ferrell taught me to be tough, patient, practical, and playful. Robert Hudspeth taught me to appreciate the power of American literature, and his example convinced me to pursue it for my career.

I am grateful to my supportive colleagues Carl Toney and Blair Wilgus for encouraging me to talk to publishers and steering me toward Mercer University Press, and to Natalie Hewitt for supporting me every step of the way. And I am indebted to the Mercer team: to Marsha Luttrell for her warm encouragement, to Patrick Jolley for his keen editing, and to Marc Jolley for his enthusiasm, wisdom, and shared love of both Hawthorne and the Hebrew Bible.

Finally, I thank my husband, Patrick Horn, for his validation, smart insights, and for reading every word.

Introduction

Prophets emerge at the beginnings of nations. In the rocky origins of ancient Israel, prophets step into the story to anoint, advise, condemn, and encourage. Prophetic literature wrestles with weighty theological issues, such as the problem of evil and the definition of righteousness. The prophets of the Hebrew Bible function as the mouthpieces of God, speaking to the people of God and to outside communities. As ancient Israel splinters and divides, her prophets seek to understand the fall of Northern Israel and the layered repercussions of that event. They address the destruction of the Jerusalem Temple, the Babylonian Exile, and the limitless challenges of restoration. They strive to understand their role in the world and their community's relationship with the Divine. In so doing, they shape the orienting narratives of the Abrahamic faiths; the voices of the prophets mold the mythology of the ancient world.

This mythology guides the Puritan narratives of its American origins, too. Just as the Israelites wander the wilderness, cross the Jordan, and arrive triumphantly in the Promised Land, Puritan pilgrims saw themselves as undertaking a Divine enterprise. They, too, crossed the perilous wilderness of the sea before arriving at last at their own "Promised Land." Thus, they aligned their journey with the ancient Israelites' journey into Canaan and the establishment of Israel. In "A Model of Christian Charity" (1630), John

Winthrop cites the very words Moses declares to the Israelites as they stand poised to enter Canaan:

> I shall shutt upp this discourse with that exhortation of Moses, that faithfull servant of the Lord, in his last farewell to Israell, Deut. 30. *Beloued there is now sett before us life and good, Death and evill, in that wee are commanded this day to loue the Lord our God, and to loue one another, to walke in his wayes and to keepe his Commandements and his Ordinance and his lawes,* and the articles of our Covenant with him, that *wee may liue and be multiplied, and that the Lord our God may blesse us in the land whither wee goe to possesse it. But if our heartes shall turne away, soe that wee will not obey, but shall be seduced, and worshipp and serue other Gods,* our pleasure and proffitts, *and serue them*; it is propounded unto us this day, *wee shall surely perishe out of the good land whither wee passe over this vast sea to possesse it;*
>
> Therefore lett us choose life
> that wee, and our seede
> may liue, by obeyeing His
> voyce and cleaveing to Him,
> for Hee is our life and
> our prosperity.

Well aware that the eyes of the world would be upon them, Winthrop urged his community to model compassionate behavior, to treat one another with the love a mother gives her child, to share in each other's burdens. His sincere use of Moses' words to the Israelites serves to reinforce this concern, but it also effectively reinforces the pilgrims' own sense that their claim on this land was divinely ordained. They were the Israelites of the New World, and the narratives of their origins were readily crafted to reflect that identity.

Enter Washington Irving, Nathaniel Hawthorne, Herman Melville, and others who, two hundred years later, sought to establish a distinctively American literature. It was around this time of course that Alexis de Tocqueville noted the lack of an American literature ("the inhabitants of the United States have then at present, properly speaking, no literature. The only authors whom I acknowledge as American are the journalists"), and what non-journalistic literature that did exist was, in essence, English:

> Not only do the Americans constantly draw upon the treasures of English literature, but it may be said with truth that they find the literature of England growing on their own soil. The larger part of that small number of men in the United States who are engaged in the composition of literary works are English in substance, and still more so in form. Thus they transport into the midst of democracy the ideas and literary fashions which are current amongst the aristocratic nation they have taken for their model. (Tocqueville, 2:13:445)

To distinguish their literature from British literature then, they would need their own founding myths and legends. A robust national literature needs narratives that gaze into the misty past as well as those that look to the future. England had King Arthur and Beowulf and Robin Hood. American writers wanted their own legends; so, they wrote them.

3

Washington Irving puts down literary American roots with tales like "Rip Van Winkle" and "The Legend of Sleepy Hollow." These first American short stories turn on their being set on American soil. Against the backdrop of the Catskill Mountains, Rip sleeps through the American revolution, waking up to find the image of King George that once hung over the inn has been replaced with one of George Washington. "The Legend of Sleepy Hollow" is also set in upstate New York and features vivid and mystery-laden depictions of this American setting as well as a pumpkin, native to north America—not England. And both stories are imbued with that ambiguous quality that makes myths and legends at once hard to put one's finger on and hard to shake from one's psyche: Could a man really sleep for twenty years? What really happened to Ichabod Crane that night?

With Irving's literary foundation laid out, Nathaniel Hawthorne crafts story after story set in the early days of Puritan New England. Interestingly, Tocqueville attributes the lack of an American literature in part to the nation's Puritan origins:

> The religion professed by the first emigrants, and bequeathed by them to their descendants, simple in its form of worship, austere and almost harsh in its principles, and hostile to external symbols and to ceremonial pomp, is naturally unfavorable to the fine arts, and only yields a reluctant sufferance to the pleasures of literature. (Tocqueville, 4:9:429)

Hawthorne, however, takes Puritan austerity as his literary starting place.

Mingling historical figures with fictional ones, Hawthorne brings a mythology of America's Puritan origins into full relief, and prophetic figures and themes figure prominently in these narratives. Hawthorne does not state explicitly that prophets are integral to his American literary project. Nevertheless, it is significant that they emerge in many his narratives set at the dawn of America, just as prophets emerge in the beginnings of ancient Israel.

Indeed, the prophetic literature of the Hebrew Bible informs Nathaniel Hawthorne's fiction. Several of Hawthorne's Puritan narratives depict prophet figures or themes associated with biblical prophecy, thus an understanding of prophetic books like Amos and Ezekiel and narratives about prophets like Moses and Elijah enhances the reading of these texts. Short stories set in Colonial New England that feature prophets include "The Gray Champion," "The Man of Adamant," "The Minister's Black Veil," and "The Gentle Boy." In brief: The Gray Champion hears the cry of an oppressed people and delivers them from oppression with a special knowledge of where true authority lies. Richard Digby of "The Man of Adamant" is an anti-prophet who draws direct comparisons with himself and the prophet Elijah, deserting his "sinful" community because he believes he alone is worthy of God's salvation. Catharine, the Quaker woman in "The Gentle Boy," enters into a trance state and utters a prophetic "woe" oracle. Reverend Hooper carries out a prophetic symbolic action in the wearing of the black veil.

Themes of prophecy pervade Hawthorne's novels as well. In *The Scarlet Letter*, Hester Prynne is a prophet along

5

the lines of Isaiah's Suffering Servant. She is rejected by her community, silently endures their criticism, but ultimately offers consolation to those who once rebuked her. *The House of the Seven Gables* opens with Matthew Maule's dark prophecy that prompts the biblical prophetic question of whether one generation inherits the sins of the previous generation. Through moments in which they engage in different kinds of prophetic revelation, the protagonists of *Seven Gables* overcome their troubled past by working toward a restoration that harmoniously incorporates past, present, and future.

In *American Prophecy: Race and Redemption in American Political Culture*, George Shulman explores the multifaceted genre that is American prophecy. He traces a spectrum of prophetic American voices (Thoreau, Douglass, King, Baldwin, Morrison), reminding us that ultimately, "Prophecy in America is thus a biblical genre, a vernacular idiom, and a political language, gripping and yet capacious, available for opposing uses. I turn to prophecy… to engage a rhetoric crucial to American life" (Shulman, x). Prophecy is not only "a rhetoric crucial to American life"; it is also foundational to the formation of American literature. As integral parts of the development of an American literary voice, prophetic themes and characters not only lend Hawthorne's tales the gravitas of a biblical narrative; they also enable Hawthorne's literature to hold the special status as being of at once creating and being of an American mythology.

In "Were It a New-Made World: Hawthorne, Melville, and the Unmasking of America," Michael Broek forwards the compelling thesis that while many who sought to create an American mythology invariably reinforced American exceptionalism, Hawthorne and Melville reject it:

> Hawthorne and Melville were among the first American imaginative writers to challenge the myth of American Exceptionalism in terms of their aesthetic operations, insofar as Hawthorne's sense of ambiguity and Melville's sense of multiple perspectives challenges the validity of any single monological narrative of national identity. (Broek, 2)

So it is on aesthetic grounds that Hawthorne's (and Melville's) texts resist American Exceptionalism. In *The Scarlet Letter*, for example, Hawthorne slaps down heavy symbols (the *A* on Hester's bosom, for example), only to reverse the assumed meaning by the end of the story. But did we ever conclusively know what it meant to begin with? And if we step back further, we find the word *adultery* never appears in the novel at all. Broek's argument is more nuanced than this, however, showing that

> the development of a context-free language—that is, a language and an idiom that is technically standardized and universally understood, but more importantly that serves to mask difference and to manufacture a (false) sense of shared destiny—has been the development of an American national mythology, and it is this mythology against which Hawthorne and Melville were the first strong American imaginative writers to place themselves, "un-masking" as it were, the false front of American Exceptionalism. (Broek, 6)

Broek is right. And for writers whose work definitively shapes America's stories about itself, it is remarkable that Hawthorne (and Melville) do not serve up heaping platefuls of American Exceptionalism. I depart from Broek in maintaining that Hawthorne does develop an American mythology; it is nuanced, and it rejects exceptionalism, but it is still a mythology of American origins. That said, part of this mythology's distinctive quality is its self-questioning, its inherent ambiguity, its depiction of major problems with its original (often Puritan) ideals. This again circles back to Broek: "Aesthetically, what Hawthorne and Melville sought was to break open old myths and symbols, many of which had become grounded in the myth of American Exceptionalism, to discover what emerged into the light, what might be found behind the 'veil'—the veil being a favorite trope of Hawthorne's" (Broek, 3). I contend that in many of Hawthorne's American origin narratives, prophets play the role of "breaking open old myths and symbols."

In light of the prophetic elements in these narratives, basic characteristics and contexts of biblical prophetic literature offer helpful background. The concept of prophecy is often misconstrued as little more than a future-telling act. However, the biblical prophets are more frequently concerned with speaking about present situations and addressing current societal issues. As the great philosopher and theologian Abraham J. Heschel writes, one of the jobs of the prophet may be "to disclose the future in order to illumine what is involved in the present" (Heschel, *The Prophets*, 12). Biblical prophets do speak of what will come to pass if a current situation is not rectified, but the focus of the prophet's message is often deeply intertwined with the prophet's present context and with persuading the community toward a particular course of action. The role of the community or audience is an essential element in prophetic literature. The way in which a community responds to the prophet's words shapes the narrative. This could be said of Hawthorne's characters too: the success of prophetic figures is determined by the extent to which the people understand them to speak the truth, whatever that may mean in the context of each narrative.

Depictions of the biblical prophets reflect a variety of socio-historical situations. The process of the composition of the Pentateuch (Exodus–Deuteronomy) and the books of the Former Prophets (Joshua–2 Kings, also known as the Deuteronomistic History) begins in the monarchy period (c. 1000 BCE) and reaches its culmination in the early Second Temple period (which begins in 536 BCE). Many of these writings exhibit the concerns and perspectives of those recovering from the aftermath of the Babylonian Exile and still striving to come to terms with the fall of Israel. Virtually all these works contain narratives about earlier times that reflect the views and biases of a community looking back on a previous period of national formation, of political unrest, or nostalgia for a time of peace and unity. Similarly, the Hawthorne narratives under consideration are retrospective: they look back to an earlier time of national formation and embody the views and biases of an early-mid nineteenth-century writer creating a national mythology imbued with shadows and ambiguity, and with which prophets are necessarily involved.

History plays a role in the choices made by writers of prophet stories. If the writer lives through a time of national division or transition, a story about a prophet who has foretold or effects change in the current crisis may offer an element of security: some controlling force, divine or otherwise, is yet in control. A story about an individual relegated to the margins of the community who grows to become a revered representative of communal identity validates the struggles undergone by those seeking to live genuinely in a difficult environment. The presence of prophets in Hawthorne's fiction offers justification for some of the various and challenging roles that individuals undertake during times of religious and or national transition. For example, prophets may seem to know more than those around them, may have a heightened sense of compassion for the oppressed, may lament the sins of the community, or may resent the perceived sinful nature of the community. And in many cases, the prophet is one whom the community doesn't fully understand. All of Hawthorne's prophets possess one or several of these characteristics.

The narratives I will explore provide a diverse cross section of prophetic themes, yet are all set—or originate, as is the case with *Seven Gables*—in the same historical context: Puritan New England. Though Hawthorne had reservations about the church in nineteenth-century America, he knew the Bible, expected his readers to know it, and wrestles with religious, and in particular Puritan, concerns in much of his literature. In general, Hawthorne seems to have subscribed to a somewhat stereotypical view of biblical prophets: they possess privileged knowledge and use that knowledge to utter prophecies of future doom for the community. Though his stories may reflect a "traditional" understanding of biblical prophecy, Hawthorne nevertheless imbues them with nuance and ambiguity, both in terms of the narrative itself and his narrative technique. Hawthorne's prophet stories play a significant role in his project of creating literary and mythic ruins that cast contrasting shadows upon American history.

Though he often wrote about early New England, Hawthorne's starting point was always nineteenth-century New England. Several different factors affected the conditions of religious life in Hawthorne's Protestant antebellum New England. New modes of post-Enlightenment thinking, advances in science, the industrial revolution, and various other developments in the early nineteenth century influenced the decline in Protestant church membership in New England and elsewhere. Some Protestant denominations joined together in an effort to renew American fidelity to the church (Albanese, *America: Religion and Religions*, 95). Yet, like several of his contemporaries, Hawthorne was largely disillusioned with the church, and wrote in 1842, "I find that my respect for clerical people, as such, and my faith in the utility of their office, decreases daily. We certainly do need a new revelation—a new system—for there seems to be no life in the old one" (Hawthorne, *The American Notebooks*, 352). Hawthorne shared with many this sense that the old forms of Protestantism were riddled with inadequacies and the need for a new way of engaging in religious experience. There was a common view in nineteenth-century America "that God, if not dead in Nietzschean terms, was somehow out of reach, no longer in this world" (Wheeler, "Love among the Ruins: Hawthorne's Surrogate Religion," 2). Though there were many church-going New Englanders, Hawthorne was not alone in his sense of detachment from the Protestantism of his day. "Hawthorne felt that a viable religion should bring the individual near to God or God near the individual, that religion should be existential rather than

11

doctrinal" (Wheeler, 2). Though Hawthorne became actively involved with the Transcendentalists for a time, living and working at the Brook Farm community, he ultimately became disillusioned with them, too. Hawthorne thus wrote during a time of religious upheaval and transition. Though flawed and often enigmatic, his literary prophets, may represent both for himself and the nation hope for religious expression during a time of such religious (and political) insecurity.

There were, however, several movements that sought to counter that insecurity. A flurry of revivalist groups endeavored to renew involvement in Protestant Christianity, many of which emphasized energetic worship and a personal relationship with God. The rise in popularity of supernaturalist phenomena such as mesmerism and spiritualism also encouraged participants to engage in rituals that lay outside of traditional worship boundaries. In addition to Transcendentalism, Hawthorne was interested in other religious groups, having considered joining a Shaker community at one time, though he disapproved of their ecstatic worship ceremonies.[1] Still, his experience with Shakerism and supernaturalism likely provided material for some of the mysterious and prophetic elements of his narratives (Masui, "Reading Haw-

---

[1] In a letter to his sister in 1831, Hawthorne writes of his visit with the Shakers: "On the whole, they lead a good and comfortable life, and if it were not for their ridiculous ceremonies, a man could not do a wiser thing than to join them. Those whom I conversed with were intelligent, and appeared happy. I spoke to them about becoming a member of the Society, but have come to no decision on that point" (Hawthorne *The Letters, 1813–1843*, 213).

thorne in the Context of the American Popular Religion,"
20). For example, the Shakers may have given him a model
for a female prophet: "The Shaker matriarch, Mother Ann
Lee, provided Hawthorne with a literary model of a prophetic woman who can be compared to Anne Hutchinson in the
colonial Massachusetts" (Masui, 25). Another influence was
his wife Sophia's interest in spiritualism and mesmerism, the
threatening presence of which we find in *The Blithedale Romance*. The nineteenth-century blend of folk supernaturalism
and Christianity also parallels the wonder lore of popular religion in colonial New England (Masui, 21). Hawthorne's
fluency in Puritan wonder lore that appears throughout *The
Scarlet Letter* and other works seems due not only to his ex-
tensive research in Puritan documents, but also to the language of popular supernaturalism of his own day.

Like the prophets of ancient Israel, Hawthorne's prophets emerge out of contexts of oppression and times of national formation. "The Gentle Boy," "The Minister's Black Veil,"
The Scarlet Letter, and *The House of the Seven Gables* all take
place or begin in the early days of Puritan New England.
These are not stories of a stable, long-established, nation.
Like the prophetic narratives connected with the origins of
Israel, Hawthorne's prophet stories tell of the start an American colony, when both the community and the young nation
are in their unstable, formative years. And, as Shulman contends, prophets set communities into motion:

> Prophets can return to origins not to fix authority
> conceived as a noun but to renew it as a verb: God
> or justice are not substances to define rightly as
> grounds of justification but commitments to risk
> and remake in action. Exercising authority not by

justifying but enacting a principle or idea, they live
by love rather than duty, surrender rather than sub-
jection, faith rather than certainty. (30)

The prophets who lead with compassion are those who bring
about positive change in Hawthorne's narratives. Movement
away from rigid ideals is central to Hawthorne's non-
exceptionalist American mythology. And the prophetic
themes and characters depicted in these narratives imbue
Hawthorne's literature of American origins with the gravitas
of biblical language and the mythical power of ambiguity.

1

The Good Prophet and the Anti-Prophet:

"The Grey Champion" and "The Man of Adamant"

"The Gray Champion" (1835) and "The Man of Adamant" (1837) feature contrasting central figures: a good prophet and an anti-prophet, respectively. "The Gray Champion" and "The Man of Adamant" serve as helpful introductory examples of Hawthorne's use of prophet figures in his narratives. They feature relatively simple primary characters who are less developed than those of other prophet stories. Whereas the Gray Champion is an ideal prophet, appearing during a crisis and delivering the oppressed, the Man of Adamant deserts his community, ultimately perishing because of his prideful delusion that he is a true prophet, alone worthy of salvation.

"The Gray Champion": The Good Prophet

In "The Gray Champion," Hawthorne sets the scene for the arrival of a prophet who will deliver his people from subjugation. The once self-ruled colonists now face domination by British rule: "James II, the bigoted successor of Charles the Voluptuous, had annulled the charters of all the colonies, and sent a harsh and unprincipled soldier to take away our liberties and endanger our religion" (9). This tyrannical leadership denies the private rights of the citizens and threatens their form of worship. The people need a leader to speak out against the British rulers and to defend the Puritan understanding of righteous religious practice. Biblical prophets are often called to eradicate or at least cry out against political and social oppression. They possess privileged knowledge of truth and justice, concern for appropriate religious practices, and the power to prophesy on these issues. The Gray Champion exhibits all these traits. He resembles Moses as the image of a mature leader with military associations, and he fits the description of the coming savior in Isaiah 19:20. Hawthorne refers to the Puritans with the biblically charged term "exiles" and uses language like that of the book of Amos with its concern for social justice. Thus, in this Puritan narrative of national formation, Hawthorne creates both the context for and the arrival of a triumphant prophet.

Hawthorne frequently alludes to prophetic contexts with the use of recognizable biblical themes and vocabulary. "The Gray Champion" conjures a familiar biblical scene: an oppressed people need deliverance from a usurping ruler who has revoked their freedoms. Amos likewise features a prophet who condemns oppressors and speaks out against the injustice wrought by those in power during an "evil time" (Amos 5:13). Amos admonishes a wealthy, controlling minority that oppress a poor, underprivileged majority. [1] The prophet addresses those powerful few:

> For I know your manifold transgressions and your mighty sins: they afflict the just, they take a bribe, and they turn aside the poor in the gate from their right. Therefore the prudent shall keep silence in that time; for it is an evil time. (Amos 5:12–13)[2]

Amos charges the wealthy Israelites with turning aside the poor and afflicting the just. He warns that Israel will fall unless the people stop worshiping in the north and return to worshiping God in the Jerusalem temple. Amos' "condemnation of the abuse of justice and wealth attempts to point to the corruption of both the religious and the political leadership of northern Israel and those in Judah who acquiesce to Israelite rule" (Sweeney, *The Twelve Prophets*, 232). Though those in power had been proud of their prosperity, Amos declares that it is actually "an evil time." In "The Gray Champion," the narrator uses this phrase as he recalls the liberties the pilgrims enjoyed before James II strove to rule the colonies: "Till these evil times, however, such allegiance had been

---

[1] For introduction to and discussion of Amos see Marvin A. Sweeney, *The Twelve Prophets*, vol. 1, 191–276.

[2] See especially 231–237 in *The Twelve Prophets*. Amos 5:1–15 uses paranesis, "a generic address form that attempts to persuade an audience to adopt a specific viewpoint or to engage in a specific course of action. In order to achieve its ends, paranesis employs both admonition, which warns the audience to avoid an undesirable course of action or point of view, and exhortation, which attempts to encourage the audience to accept a desirable course of action or point of view" (231).

merely nominal, and the colonists had ruled themselves, enjoying far more freedom, than is even yet the privilege of the native subjects of Great Britain" (9–10).[3] In Hawthorne's text, those early days when the people governed themselves has a mythic quality; America began with a kind of freedom that surpasses even that of contemporary British citizens. These idyllic origins contrast sharply with "these evil times" of domineering British rule.[4] This prophetic phrase conjures something between a biblical and mythic tone that helps establish a context in which the services of a prophet, leader, or champion will be required.

Many prophetic texts depict an oppressed or exiled people seeking deliverance from corrupt rulers. Hawthorne echoes this trope with his use of the word, "exiles" to describe the earliest Puritan settlers in "The Gray Champion": "Indeed, it was not yet time for the old spirit to be extinct; since there were men in the street, that day, who had worshiped there beneath the trees, before a house was reared to the God, for whom they had become exiles" (11). Hawthorne aligns the Massachusetts colony with the Israelites insofar as colonists left their homeland because of their faithfulness to God. Throughout their writings, the Puritan settlers regularly cast themselves as Israelites struggling and alone in the

---

[3] Nathaniel Hawthorne, *Twice Told Tales. Edited by William Charvat, et al. Columbus: Ohio State University Press, 1965.*

[4] Contrasting the time when the people governed themselves with that of an oppressive ruler has other biblical resonances, such as with 1 Samuel 8, which tells of the origin of the Israelite monarchy when the people called for a king despite the prophet Samuel's assurance that the only leader they need is God.

wilderness, seeking the Promised Land, or exiled from their homeland. In such a context, Hawthorne understands that they would need the guidance of a prophet who can speak on their behalf.

Several biblical prophets describe, or themselves serve as, the leaders who deliver their people or sometimes the people of other nations. Isaiah 19 depicts the punishment and subsequent redemption Egypt will undergo at the hand of the God of Israel, The Lord of Hosts.[5] Though the act of sending a leader to deliver non-Israelites is not a regular occurrence, the lines in Isaiah 19:20 (KJV)[6] resonate with Hawthorne's story: "And it shall be for a sign and for a witness unto the LORD of hosts in the land of Egypt: for they shall cry unto the LORD because of the oppressors, and he shall send them a saviour, and a great one, and he shall deliver them." Isaiah prophecies that the people will cry out for someone to deliver them from oppression, and that God will hear that cry and send a savior to them. As the rest of chapter 19 suggests, all of Egypt—and Assyria—will eventually earn the protection of The Lord of Hosts. Using the same

---

[5] See Marvin A. Sweeney, *Isaiah 1-39*, 263–275. The future-oriented event in this passage offers "direction for understanding the purpose of the current chaos in Egypt. As such, they indicate that Egyptian internal conflict is not only caused by YHWH but serves YHWH's intention to realize blessing in the land involving Israel, Egypt, and Assyria" (268).

[6] All biblical quotations are from the King James (Authorized Version) Bible unless otherwise noted.

title for God as do Isaiah and many other biblical prophets,[7] an unnamed individual in "The Gray Champion" calls for deliverance: "'Oh! Lord of Hosts,' cried a voice among the crowd, 'provide a Champion for thy people!'" (13).[8] The language of deliverance pervades Hawthorne's story. Once the mysterious leader appears, the people "raised a shout of awe and exultation, and looked for the deliverance of New England" (15). Like the oppressed Israelite voices throughout prophetic and other biblical texts, these early Americans cry to be delivered.[9]

Yet for all his parallels with a prophetic figure, the Gray Champion is called a "Champion," not a prophet. The word, "champion," occurs three times throughout the entire King James Bible, and all three times it describes one man: Goliath. "And there went out a champion out of the camp of the

---

[7] Incidentally, this title never occurs in the New Testament; it is strictly a Hebrew Bible title for God, e.g., "As for our redeemer, the LORD of hosts is his name, the Holy One of Israel (Isaiah 47:4).

[8] Though prophetic texts regularly depict or foretell deliverance, individuals or groups calling out for deliverance occurs frequently throughout the body of the Psalms as well. For example: "O Lord my God, in thee I do put my trust: save me from all them that persecute me, and deliver me" (7:1), "Deliver me from mine enemies, O my God: defend me from them that rise up against me" (59:1), "Deliver me, O LORD, from mine enemies: I flee unto thee to hide me" (143:9).

[9] Somewhat like the context of rebellion out of which the Gray Champion emerges, a probable setting for the composition of the Isaian passage was "the revolt of the northern kingdom of Israel against Assyria in 724–21" (Sweeney, *Isaiah 1-39*, 271).

The Good Prophet and the Anti-Prophet

Philistines, named Goliath, of Gath" (1 Samuel 17:4). Goliath does serve his people, and he is distinguished by military prowess rather than prophetic abilities. But of course, he is not an Israelite; he represents the enemy. Indeed, his defeat by the young David marks a triumph for the Israelite people. Though the allusion is qualified, Goliath's status as a great warrior lends itself to the image of Hawthorne's Gray Champion who is likewise depicted as a great, though aged, military hero.

Both military ad religious leader, the Gray Champion is "fit either to rule a host in the battle-field or be raised to God in prayer" (15). Moses, the first and greatest prophet according to Deuteronomy 34:10-12,[10] functions also as priest, judge, lawgiver, and military leader as he delivers his people from bondage in Egypt and leads them to the Promised Land. Moses "plays an important role in battle, much as a Levitical priest would accompany soldiers in war (Exod 17; Deut 20)" (Sweeney, *The Prophetic Literature*, 29). Similarly, the Gray Champion is associated with battle, yet does not actually fight. Thus, the multifaceted career of Moses serve in some ways as a model for the mysterious Gray Champion who likewise delivers his people from oppression during a time of national formation, and who deals out justice as might a military leader. Like the Gray Champion, Moses

---

[10] "And there arose not a prophet since in Israel like unto Moses, whom the LORD knew face to face, In all the signs and the wonders, which the LORD sent him to do in the land of Egypt to Pharaoh, and to all his servants, and to all his land, And in all that mighty hand, and in all the great terror which Moses shewed in the sight of all Israel" (Deuteronomy 34:10–12).

also establishes the law. Serving as a mediator between God and the people, "Moses purposes to explain what Yahweh has commanded (1:5). Thus Moses is not only a lawgiver: he becomes the law's interpreter" (Beegle 915). Moreover, Moses continues to serve his people with energy and clarity even in his old age: "And Moses was an hundred and twenty years old when he died: his eye was not dim, nor his natural force abated" (Deuteronomy 34:7).[11] The picture of the ancient but vigorous Moses is not unlike the image of the powerful but very gray champion, "displaying a face of antique majesty, rendered doubly venerable by the hoary beard that descended on his breast" (14). Aged yet powerful, the Gray Champion, like Moses, acts in the office of lawgiver and military leader.

While the Gray Champion heralds promise, his arrival signifies a time of struggle: "Long, long may it be, ere he comes again! His hour is one of darkness, and adversity, and peril." The mysterious Gray Champion is an old, bearded man with wisdom, military prowess, and religious authority. He delivers his community in part by possessing special knowledge, namely, that the tyrannical king is no longer on

---

[11] The narrative description of Moses as powerful contrasts with Moses' own estimation of his abilities in Deuteronomy 31:2: "And he said unto them, I am an hundred and twenty years old this day; I can no more go out and come in: also the LORD hath said unto me, Thou shalt not go over this Jordan." The text offers a "paradoxical portrait of Moses as both a strong, heroic prophet and fragile mortal…At the point of narrating Moses' human frailty and limits at his death, the narrative also lifts up his closeness to God in both relationship and power" (Olson, "Moses," 150).

the throne back in England. In keeping with much of the biblical prophetic literature, this prophecy is not so much about the future, as it is an understanding of the present that points to an altered future. The Gray Champion declares:

> And what speak ye of James? There is no longer a popish tyrant on the throne of England, and by tomorrow noon, his name shall be a by-word in this very street, where ye would make it a word of terror. Back, thou that wast a Governor, back![12] With this night thy power is ended—tomorrow, the prison!—back, lest I fortel the scaffold! (16)

Verbally powerful and authoritative, the Gray Champion has dethroned the Governor with words and knowledge of the political turnover in England. He asserts with authority where the real power lies and where it does not, a concern typical of biblical prophets. Like Amos and others, the Gray Champion distinguishes rightful, appropriately powerful rulers from those whose "authority" is not sanctioned by God.

With these words to the governor, the pompous British oppressors retreat, and the prophet soon disappears. Though it is said that he will return in future times of great need, just as tales have been told of his appearance during significant

---

[12] The line, "back thou that wast a Governor!" could be reminiscent of Jesus asserting his authority over demoniacs and betrayers, as in Matthew 16:32: "But he turned, and said unto Peter, Get thee behind me, Satan: thou art an offence unto me: for thou savourest not the things that be of God, but those that be of men." Jesus has the prophetic ability to know the truths behind the superficial words of those he encounters.

battles for the independence of America. In this way, the Gray Champion assumes the character of a mythic figure as he, prophet-like, appears in times of need. In Malachi's prophecy of Elijah, the final words of the prophetic writings and indeed the entire (Protestant) Hebrew Bible, God declares, "Behold, I will send you Elijah the prophet before the coming of the great and dreadful day of the LORD: And he shall turn the heart of the fathers to the children, and the heart of the children to their fathers, lest I come and smite the earth with a curse" (Malachi 4:5–6). Prophets rarely come forth to declare that everything is going well and to keep up the good work. They come forth to evince change: to condemn religious sinners and social oppressors, to advocate justice, to assert where true authority lies, and to provide hope for the righteous. The Gray Champion is such a prophet.

"The Man of Adamant": The Anti-Prophet

Richard Digby is the only one of Hawthorne's Puritan characters who actually considers himself in league with the biblical prophets. Yet, he is the furthest thing from one. The antithesis of the Gray Champion, Digby condemns righteous people, has no interest in helping others, and is completely deluded in thinking he alone possesses knowledge of religious truth. At the end of the story, Hawthorne contrasts him with Mary Goffe, who typifies "pure religion" (168), and functions as a real prophet, foreseeing his deadly fate and offering him salvation. Her example of prophetic goodness confirms Digby as an anti-prophet, a literary contrast that further demonstrates Hawthorne's use of prophets as enigmatic yet heroic.

There is no ambiguity in the misanthropic character of Richard Digby. In the first sentence, we learn that Digby is "the gloomiest and most intolerant of a stern brotherhood" (161). Digby views himself as the only person who will be saved amidst a world of sinners. Hawthorne's romantic, stylized language sets the moralizing, but somewhat satirical, tone of his apologue: "His plan of salvation was so narrow, that, like a plank in a tempestuous sea, it could avail no sinner but himself, who bestrode it triumphantly, and hurled anathemas against the wretches whom he saw struggling with the billows of eternal death" (161). Digby has nothing of the darkly attractive if flawed quality of many of Hawthorne's other Puritan characters. He falls at the bleakest end of the spectrum of ministerial prophet characters, and he is the least enigmatic, which, in a way, is the heart of his problem. He is completely isolated from his community, viewing himself as possessing special knowledge about salvation that absolutely no one else is privy to. He does not undergo any kind of mental or emotional inner struggle as does Hester Prynne, nor does he long to be valued by those around him as does Reverend Hooper. A truer prophet would see the potential salvation of their community, or at least sincerely lament their damnation. But Richard Digby views others as incapable of righteousness and therefore his only hope to secure his own salvation is to curse them and remove himself from their presence.

Richard Digby uses biblical language and allusion to align himself with the isolated righteous man who finds himself forced to walk amongst sinners. The title of the story itself may allude to Ezekiel 3:9, in which God declares to the prophet Ezekiel, "As an adamant harder than flint have I made thy forehead: fear them not, neither be dismayed at their looks, though they be a rebellious house." In the context of this verse, Ezekiel's own community, the House of Israel, has been rebellious and disobedient, and God charges Ezekiel to address them regarding their sinful behavior. Richard Digby may *think* of himself as an Ezekiel, whose community has sinned against God. But Digby rejects his people thereby showing that he has not a forehead, but heart of adamant. Digby justifies his removal from them with allusion to Psalm 120:5, which reads, "Woe is me, that I sojourn in Mesech, that I dwell in the tents of Kedar!" Digby's reference to this psalm is laced with sweeping biblical overtones: "Peradventure, were I to tarry longer in the tents of Kedar, the gracious boon would be revoked, and I also be swallowed up in the deluge of wrath, or consumed in the storm of fire and brimstone, or involved in whatever new kind of ruin is ordained for the horrible perversity of this generation" (161–162). In addition to using the language of the King James Bible, Digby also takes up typical biblical themes that prophets are often concerned with, such as the sins of the generations, the imagery of deluge, and talk of fire and brimstone. Of course, Digby recklessly skews his interpretation of the prophetic narratives. Digby's self-centered worldview and misconstrued use of biblical language is another way in which Hawthorne paints a picture of the worst embodiment of a prophet.

Hawthorne's narration also echoes prophet narratives with his uses of isolated wanderer language, a genre common to biblical prophetic literature that we find in such narratives as those of Moses and Elijah: "So Richard Digby took an axe, to hew space enough for a tabernacle in the wilderness..." (162). This sentence that began as a narrative that sounds biblical, takes a disquieting turn: "...and some few other necessaries, especially a sword and gun, to smite and slay any intruder upon his hallowed seclusion" (162). Though the tabernacles of the Bible are places of worship for the righteous people of God, not sinners, the biblical prophet seeks to lead people toward righteousness so that they will be welcome in the tabernacle. In Exodus, Moses sets up the tabernacle at some distance from the camp, just as Digby sets up his "tabernacle" far away from the town. Yet Moses' tabernacle is intended to be a sanctuary for many, not for a single individual: "And it came to pass, that every one which sought the LORD went out unto the tabernacle of the congregation, which was without the camp" (Exodus 33:7b). The title of the sanctuary, "the tabernacle of the congregation," implies the communal nature of the place of worship.[13]

Digby's plan to murder anyone who invades his secluded tabernacle also stands in clear contradiction with the prophet Ezekiel's vision of restoration in which God states that the tabernacle will stand forever in the midst of the people:

> Moreover I will make a covenant of peace with them; it shall be an everlasting covenant with them: and I will place them, and multiply them, and will set my sanctuary in the midst of them for evermore. My tabernacle also shall be with them: yea, I will be

---

[13] See also Exodus 29:43 and 35:21 regarding the communal nature of the tabernacle.

their God, and they shall be my people. And the heathen shall know that I the LORD do sanctify Israel, when my sanctuary shall be in the midst of them for evermore. (Ezekiel 37:26–28)

Ezekiel's vision of restoration suggests that when the right relationship with God has been restored, the tabernacle will remain amid the people. By contrast, Digby's exclusive tabernacle suggests a broken relationship with God. Hawthorne characterizes Digby as an anti-prophet by beginning a biblical allusion—the making of a tabernacle set at a distance from the community—and then perverting it by stating that Digby stocks it with weapons in order to slay anyone who attempts to enter his private shrine.

Continuing the theme of the wandering holy man, Digby compares himself to a biblical prophet through an allusion to Elijah wandering in a sinful land: Digby "journeyed onward three days and two nights, and came, on the third evening, to the mouth of a cave, which, at first sight, reminded him of Elijah's cave at Horeb, though perhaps it more resembled Abraham's sepulchral cave, at Machpelah." The reference to Elijah's cave at Horeb alludes to 1 Kings 19 in which Elijah comes upon a cave away from the city full of sinners that is ruled by Ahab and Jezebel. God appears to Elijah and asks him why he is there, to which Elijah replies, "I have been very jealous for the LORD God of hosts: for the children of Israel have forsaken thy covenant, thrown down thine altars, and slain thy prophets with the sword; and I, even I only, am left; and they seek my life, to take it away" (1 Kings 19:10). According to the 1 Kings narrator, Elijah believes himself to be the only righteous one out of the midst of the sinful children of Israel.[14] Digby imagines he, like Elijah, is the only righteous individual out of a community of sinners, but Hawthorne corrects him. While Digby fancies he has arrived at his own cave of Horeb, the narrator modifies this, foreshadowing instead that it is more appropriately the tomb of Abraham (Genesis 25:9; 50:13). Like Abraham's sepulcher at Machpelah, Digby's cave will be his tomb, not the place where he will receive revelation from God. All of Hawthorne's prophets are isolated from the community in some way. But in his pride, Digby sees himself as on a par with Elijah at Horeb, which further separates him from the biblical prophets and those in Hawthorne's other narratives.

Indeed, Digby's actions both allude to and contrast with those of true prophets. Elijah and Moses are also depicted as somewhat isolated figures, retreating alone to encounter God on mountains. Not unlike Hawthorne's Richard Digby, Elijah "isolates himself on a mountain as an oracular diviner (2 Kings 1), and he spares no efforts in his oracular criticism of King Ahab and Queen Jezebel of Israel (1 Kings 21) and their son Ahaziah (2 Kings 1)" (Sweeney, *The Prophetic Literature*, 31). The Man of Adamant takes on and exaggerates this kind of prophetic persona, viewing himself as surrounded by heathens, and ultimately isolating himself deep in the woods. But Hawthorne emphasizes the darkness of the forest

---

[14] From Elijah's perspective, he is the only righteous Israelite. Yet it might be said that God corrects Elijah on this point too when God states, "Yet I have left me seven thousand in Israel, all the knees which have not bowed unto Baal, and every mouth which hath not kissed him" (1 Kings 19:18).

that Digby descends into, rather than depicting him as climbing some lofty peak, as do the biblical prophets with which he identifies.

When the apparition of Mary Goffe offers Digby a chance at salvation, she alludes to Ezekiel. Mary prophesies, "Do this, and thy stony heart shall become softer than a babe's and all will be well" (167). Mary utters the first positive allusion to prophetic literature. Her words echo God's affirmation to Israel spoken through Ezekiel: "I will take away the stony heart out of your flesh, and I will give you an heart of flesh" (Ezekiel 36:26). Though the Israelites have sinned and become unclean, God will cleanse them and will give them new hearts and through this will reestablish a relationship with them. Speaking the words of a true prophet, Mary Goffe is the compassionate counter to the bitter Richard Digby. Whereas Digby perverts the previous prophetic allusions, Mary's are faithful. She is a vision of ideal womanhood, delicate, beautiful, and good, "like a sorrowing angel" (167). However, Mary Goffe is also non-human; she—somewhat like Dante's Beatrice—is either a "ghost that haunted the wild forest, or else a dreamlike spirit, typifying pure Religion" (167–168). A good prophet, Mary shares characteristics with the Gray Champion: she possesses special knowledge (that Digby's heart is turning to stone), offers him guidance toward physical and spiritual salvation, and she is evanescent, seeming to appear in this world from an alternate physical sphere.[15]

---

[15] Mary can also be viewed as both a Christ and a Madonna figure. She bears the name of the divine Mother and grieves like her when Digby refuses her offer of rebirth. There are also sugges-

Ironically, it was Richard Digby who initially converted Mary Goffe: "She had been a convert to his preaching of the word in England, before he yielded himself to that exclusive bigotry which now enfolded him with such an iron grasp that no other sentiment could reach his bosom" (165). It seems he once was a good religious leader, but in the ultimate act that seals his fate and confirms his status as an anti-prophet, Digby curses Mary and rejects her offer of salvation. His final words are a paragon of exclusivism: "What hast thou to do with my Bible?—what with my prayers?—what with my heaven?" (167). That which a real prophet would endeavor to make available to all, Digby sees as his alone. His determination to defend to the death his private tabernacle and his private heaven results in his own death. As Digby turns to stone, Mary's spirit dissolves into the sunshine. If anyone is like Elijah, it is she: ascending to heaven as on a fiery chariot.[16] And Digby, acting out of his totally deluded worldview, has rejected his community, condemned the righteous spirit of Mary Goffe, and thus secured his place in stone and local legend as the embodiment of an anti-prophet.

Featuring characters on opposing ends of a spectrum, "The Gray Champion" (1835) and "The Man of Adamant"

---

tions of Christ imagery in the thorns and her wounded feet (Gracia Fay Ellwood, 10 January 2010).

[16] Elijah's purity is such that he does not die as a regular mortal, but is lifted off the earth and carried directly to heaven: "And it came to pass, as they still went on, and talked, that, behold, there appeared a chariot of fire, and horses of fire, and parted them both asunder; and Elijah went up by a whirlwind into heaven" (2 Kings 2:11).

(1837) introduce and illustrate the presence of prophets in Hawthorne's fiction. The Gray Champion is the paragon of a prophet, and Richard Digby displays all that which a good prophet is not. The ensuing chapters begin more detailed explorations of prophecy in "The Gentle Boy" (1831), "The Minister's Black Veil" (1836), *The Scarlet Letter* (1850), and *The House of the Seven Gables* (1851). Catharine is the passionate prophet of "The Gentle Boy." Uttering a prophetic woe oracle to the Puritans, she cries out against the oppression of her people from the margins of society. Reverend Hooper of "The Minister's Black Veil" likewise dwells on the fringes of communal acceptance. His wearing a forbidding veil over his face, like a biblical prophet carrying out a symbolic action, invites a provocative speculation on human response to mystery. Hester Prynne of *The Scarlet Letter* is Boston's own suffering servant. Like the enigmatic figure from the book of Isaiah, Hester withstands countless attacks, but ultimately comes to serve as the wonderful counselor of her generation. The prophetic theme of inherited sin shapes *The House of the Seven Gables*, and it is through moments of temporal transcendence that the protagonists achieve a kind of restoration from the Puritan prophecy.

Abraham Heschel reminds us that the prophet's job is to stop society in its tracks: "the prophet was an individual who said No to his society, condemning its habits and assumptions, its complacency, waywardness, and syncretism. He was often compelled to proclaim the very opposite of what his heart expected" (Heschel, *The Prophets*, xix). Each of Hawthorne's prophets does this in some way: the Gray Champion says No to the English authorities; Richard Digby self-defeatingly rejects the community that would have accepted

32

him; Catharine calls for an end to the oppression of Quakers; Reverend Hooper refuses to remove the veil; Hester Prynne, through her compassionate service, ultimately revokes the community's condemnation of her as a sinner; and the protagonists of *The House of the Seven Gables* say No to Maule's curse, transcending the complacency of accepting inherited sin.

Rejecting communal habits and proclaiming the opposite of how the heart may want to act jars both the prophet and the prophet's community. The prophet often has the difficult task of opening the hearts of the people, which necessarily involves an increased awareness of uncomfortable or painful realities. To this effect, Heschel speaks of Jeremiah's capacity to appreciate the pain of and the compassion needed to proclaim (or enact) the prophetic message:

> The prophet is prepared for pain. One of the effects of his presence is to intensify the people's capacity for suffering, to rend the veil that lies between life and pain. And yet Jeremiah knew how shattering the outpouring of God's anger could be. "Chastise, O Lord, but in just measure; not in Thy anger, lest Thou bring me to nothing" (Jeremiah 12:24). (179)

Such an awareness of pain characterizes all of Hawthorne's prophets, but they vary in the degree to which they exhibit compassion. This is key to the changes they bring about in their communities. Ultimately, the more Hawthorne's prophets exercise compassion, the greater their ability to effect restoration.

2

The Passionate Prophet:
Catharine of "The Gentle Boy"

"The Gentle Boy" was Hawthorne's most popular tale during his lifetime. It was also one of his earliest and most revised stories (first published in *The Token* in 1831). Though the work was well loved by his friends and family, Hawthorne viewed this early piece as highly flawed. In his introduction to a special edition from 1839, *The Gentle Boy: A Thrice-Told Tale*, Hawthorne remarks that there are few of his stories "which, on reperusal, affect him less painfully with a sense of imperfect and ill-wrought conception than 'The Gentle Boy.' But the opinion of many...compels him to the conclusion that nature here led him deeper into the Universal heart than Art has been able to follow" (Crowley, *Hawthorne: The Critical Heritage*, 68).

Despite his reservations about "The Gentle Boy," Hawthorne consents that the work accesses universal truths. At the very least, it sets into motion elements of a plot that would resurface again and again in Hawthorne's tales of colonial New England. Frederick Newberry, in "The Biblical Veil: Sources and Typology in Hawthorne's 'The Minister's

Black Veil,'" asserts that "The Gentle Boy" serves as a template for Hawthorne's subsequent Puritan narratives: "All of Nathaniel Hawthorne's historical tales of seventeenth-century New England are patterned along lines first developed in 'The Gentle Boy'" (Newberry, 363). Newberry suggests that one of these lines is "the historical struggle between Puritans and their opponents," or, more abstractly, "between Puritan absolutism and moderation" (363). Secondly, Newberry argues that a central figure representing such moderation can be found in all the Puritan tales:

> Hawthorne insinuates in every tale one or two figures whose function it is to show a possible mediation of the larger historical struggle. Endowed with piety, reason, gentleness, or sympathy, these figures stand in passive or oppressed opposition to the main contenders and, because they lack sufficient strength, come to symbolize recessive forces in New England history. (363)

Though such figures are more the stuff of Hawthorne's creative imagination than characters based in historical research, they offer a waning hope in the midst of bleak colonial extremes. They "posit the likelihood that there were once potential alternatives to narrow Puritan rule. Of course, these mediating figures are overpowered or destroyed by Puritan severity and persecution. And with their demise, salutary alternatives in New England history disappear. Their loss is the tragedy of Hawthorne's Puritan drama" (363). The argument for such figures in Hawthorne's Puritan narratives opens the discussion to the presence of other character types that act in the tragedy of Hawthorne's Puritan drama. Making a regular appearance in this drama is the prophet figure.

Unlike Newberry's figure of moderation, the Hawthornian prophet rarely assumes a moderate stance in the Puritan narrative. The prophet of "The Gentle Boy" is Catharine, the Quaker extremist. She operates as a catalyst for the dramatic scenes of the story, and in her radical plight to fight Puritan oppression, her vulnerabilities show around the edges. If "The Gentle Boy" does indeed lay the groundwork for subsequent Puritan narratives, then a prophet figure, as represented in this tale by Catharine, is a regular part of that narrative groundwork that supports many of Hawthorne's other Puritan stories. In "The Gentle Boy," Hawthorne imbues Catharine with the effects of biblical prophets, such as the "woe" speech she howls at the Puritan congregation, and her passionate dedication to delivering her people from oppression. Hawthorne's characterization of Catharine lends a mythic authority to the tensions in the text represented by the Quakers and the Puritans. Central among these tensions are the oppression wrought by the Puritans upon the Quakers and the fanatic response of the Quakers to that oppression. These qualities lend gravity to the tightly intertwined relationship between oppression and fanaticism.

Additionally, Catharine shows her passion with the use of prophetic language. She justly condemns the Puritans for killing her husband and banishing her; however, the narrator criticizes her for the personal nature of her prophetic utterance. He also condemns her fanaticism that prompts her to choose activism over her own son. Yet in so doing, she stands in the tradition of biblical prophets who fight for their understanding of the truth over and above earthly ties or social acceptance. Catharine is caught in a paradox: the prophet who seeks the community's redemption must be cut off from that community. In this she resembles many a biblical prophet. Yet her lack of tenderness curbs the restoration she can affect. At the end of the story, Catharine reports King Charles' decision to ban the persecution of the Quakers, but there is no indication that her activism played a role in bringing this about. It is the suffering and death of the gentle boy, the embodiment of unconditional compassion, whose spirit ultimately brings about a gradual softening of the hearts of the Puritan community.

When we first encounter Catharine, she fits a biblical description of one engaged in repentance or mourning: she looks wild, has ashes in her hair, and "a shapeless robe of sackcloth was girded about her waist with a knotted cord" (81). Even Hawthorne's word choice echoes biblical language. (Antiquated words such as "sackcloth" and "girded" occur regularly in the King James translation of the Bible, with which Hawthorne and his contemporaries were familiar.[1]) The imagery of sackcloth and ashes in Hebrew Bible

---

[1] In his 1941 article, "The Sources and Themes of Hawthorne's 'The Gentle Boy,' G. Harrison Orians cites William Sewel's *The History of the Rise, Increase, and Progress of the Christian People Called Quakers* as a primary source for the descriptions and experiences of the Quakers in the tale. Catharine's character and actions, such as wearing sackcloth and making proclamations, was likely drawn from the lives of Quaker women described in Sewel, among other documents. The most direct sources for the image of a woman dressed in sackcloth and interrupting a Puritan gathering are actual Puritan and Quaker documents that depict several such instances. Orians notes that, "Presumably Hawthorne was familiar

narratives represent mourning and repentance. The general idea behind this physical transformation is that the individual neglects or soils the body to represent the low state of the one who has sinned, suffered a great loss, or who wishes to gain favor with the divine. Although the wearing of sackcloth and ashes in the Hebrew Bible does not necessarily conjure images of prophets, sackcloth is sometimes donned in response to a prophet's words, as in Jonah.[2] In 1 Kings 20:35–43, an unnamed man who is "of the prophets" (41) disguises himself with ashes, but his doing so is not directly connected with his office as a prophet. The prophet Daniel

---

with the story of Margaret Brewster, who marched into the Old South Church in 1677 dressed in sackcloth, with ashes upon her head and her face blackened" (674). Hawthorne drew heavily from early documents for his Puritan stories, and the image of a woman dressed in sackcloth and speaking out against a perceived disorder may derive more from these early documents than from the biblical precedent. Yet, as Orians also notes, "it is probably true that any attendant of a New England church in the nineteenth century would have heard enough of Old Testament 'sackcloth and ashes' to have needed no historical incident" (n 674).

[2] There is one direct connection between sackcloth and prophecy in the New Testament. In Revelation, the angel figure declares, "And I will give power unto my two witnesses, and they shall prophesy a thousand two hundred and threescore days, clothed in sackcloth" (11:3). For more on sackcloth, see "Cloth, Clothes" in *The New Interpreter's Dictionary of the Bible*, Vol. 1: "Sackcloth was considered the principal garment for mourners and those displaying their repentance (Matt 11:21). Thus, it is mentioned in the Jonah narrative as the universal garment worn by the fasting people and animals of Nineveh, as a sign of repentance and mourning for their misdeeds (Jonah 3:7-8)" (695).

wears sackcloth and ashes as a part of confessing his sinfulness, and that of his community, to God: "And I set my face unto the Lord God, to seek by prayer and supplication, with fasting, and sackcloth, and ashes: And I prayed unto the LORD my God, and made my confession" (Daniel 9:3–4a). Repentance is a common aim for the wearing of sackcloth and ashes. They represent a physical show of humility before God and the hope of restoration. Catharine's wearing of sackcloth and ashes gives her the quality of a biblical personage who is denying physical (and familial) comforts or obligations in an effort to gain such a restoration.

While Hawthorne's Catharine does not seek repentance—indeed that may be her central flaw—she is certainly in a state of anguish.[3] On one level, Hawthorne seems to have clothed Catharine in ashes and sackcloth to create a biblical image of a religious outsider. For Hawthorne, the wearing of sackcloth appears to characterize one who is out of touch with the community and engaged in an extreme form of religious demonstration. To be sure, this is the case when an individual or community engages in mourning or repentance in the Hebrew Bible. One biblical example of a woman wearing ashes as a symbol as her detachment from the community comes from the narrative of the rape of Tamar in 2 Samuel 13. Tamar puts ashes on her head after she has just been raped and discarded by her half-brother, Amnon: "And Tamar put ashes on her head, and rent her garment of divers colors that was on her, and laid her hand

---

[3] In *The Province of Piety: Moral History in Hawthorne's Early Tales*, Michael Colacurcio posits that human nature never fully transforms in Hawthorne's Puritan narratives (175).

on her head, and went on crying" (2 Sam 13:19). She does not wear sackcloth, but she tears her special garment that once signified her status as a virgin princess. Weeping accompanies the wearing of ashes and tearing of her garment. These actions represent mourning on several levels. Tamar mourns for the loss of her status as a virgin, for the wretched violation that was just forced upon her by her own half-brother, and for his subsequent rejection of her. These gestures also represent the loss of order and of appropriate familial relationship that the rape and rejection embody. Because the "friend" who advises Amnon to rape his sister is described as "very wise" (חָכָם מְאֹד *hakam meod*) and Tamar, the only individual in this narrative who actually speaks wisdom, is rejected, Tamar's mourning is also a response to this chaos and disorder.[4] She reacts not only to her personal vio-

---

[4] Meir Sternberg's concept of gapping and especially of repetition—the idea that the omniscient narrator has purposefully applied systems of repetition and redundancy in the telling of the story to engage the audience in the drama of reading—highlights the emphasis on Amnon's foolishness and Tamar's wisdom in 2 Samuel 13:1–19. See Meir Sternberg, *The Poetics of Biblical Narrative: Ideological Literature and the Drama of Reading*. The frequent recurrence of references to eyes and seeing, especially in connection with the lustful, unprincipled Amnon, drips with irony. Vision is generally associated with wisdom, and we find several references to it in many wisdom texts. The author seems to have consciously chosen to repeat references to eyes and seeing to emphasize Amnon's figurative blindness. Repetition occurs again in Tamar's response to Amnon's first entreat to have her lie with him, when she speaks four negations in reply to Amnon's proposition. In addition to not wanting to be raped by her own half-

lation and abuse, but also to a world in which those who are in power abuse that power to corrupt and oppress. As is the case in "The Gentle Boy," familial and religious boundaries are violated in a strained society. Catharine makes a physical demonstration of the fact that family boundaries have been violated in ways that are utterly irreparable. Tamar cannot get her virginity back, nor can Catharine get her executed husband back. Both demonstrate this through verbal condemnation of how they were treated and the physical symbols of spiritual distress.

As with Catharine's wearing of sackcloth and ashes, the trance state she enters heightens the biblical overtones of her prophetic utterance. In the Hebrew Bible, and indeed throughout the ancient near east, there were different kinds of prophets. For example, Egyptian prophets were known for interpreting dreams and composing poetry, while many Mesopotamian prophets frequently read omens and divined oracles. From ancient Mesopotamian literature we also learn about the *muhhu*, or "ecstatic" prophet, who is described as having entered into "trance possession, including irrational acts such as the drawing of his own blood, to deliver rational oracles on behalf of the deity that he represented" (Sweeney, *The Prophetic Literature* 26).[5] A familiar example of this kind

---

brother, Tamar is also able to move beyond her immediate situation to warn Amnon of the repercussions his act would have in their socio-cultural sphere, for her, as well as for him. In tearing her garment and covering herself wish ashes she mourns these violations as well as her own.

[5] While there were female prophets, it is assumed that the *muhhu* were generally male.

of trance possession in the Hebrew Bible is a negative one: Elijah's encounter with the prophets of Baal at Mount Carmel in 1 Kings 18. The prophets of Baal are depicted as going into ecstatic trance states, dancing, and drawing blood.[6] Catharine also goes into a trance state to give her prophetic pronouncement. If Catharine is a prophetess, she, like the prophets of Baal on Mount Carmel, is one who misses the mark, who relies on primitive ritual rather than "appropriate" channels for communicating a divine message. While her ecstatic behavior initially brings forth beauty, it ultimately compromises her credibility once she yields to anger and bitterness.

Though biblical prophets engaged in numerous forms of activities and writings, they were, above all else, speakers. Catharine's significant prophetic declaration is the *woe oracle* she delivers to the Puritan congregation in her trance state. In the biblical prophetic context, "an oracle is a divine communication presented through an intermediary such as a priest, prophet, or seer. It may be delivered in response to an inquiry...or it may be unsolicited" (Sweeney, *The Prophetic Literature* 37). The *woe* formula of the oracle stands among the most basic forms of biblical prophetic communication. The condemnatory content and repetition of *woe* in Catharine's speech aligns it closely with the biblical woe oracle. The word, *woe*, is the translation of the Hebrew expression, *hoy* (הוֹי), an exclamation of lament. The general purpose of the woe oracle in prophetic literature is "to criticize specific

---

[6] For more on ancient near eastern ecstatic ritual see Marvin Sweeney, *I & II Kings: A Commentary*, 228.

actions and attitudes of people, and to announce punishment against them" (Sweeney, *The Prophetic Literature* 41). Biblical scholars identify the woe oracle through its two basic elements: "(1) the introductory exclamation *hoy*, followed by a participle or a noun that describes the action or people in question; and (2) additional material employing various forms to elaborate upon the situation" (Sweeney, *The Prophetic Literature* 41).[7] Understanding the nature and purposes of the woe oracle enhances our analysis of Catharine's dramatic speech, which employs this biblical formula.[8]

---

[7] See also Marvin Sweeney, *Isaiah 1-39: With an Introduction to Prophetic Literature*, 543.

[8] W. R. Thompson offers a thorough, if sometimes rather pat, treatment of Hawthorne's biblical references in his 1962 article, "Patterns of Biblical Allusions in Hawthorne's 'The Gentle Boy.'" His basic premise is that the biblical allusions in the narrative are more than "an unconscious by-product of [Hawthorne's] known familiarity with the Bible" (9). Thompson sees New Testament references dominating the text, and that the author's use of biblical allusions form "a highly complex literary method" (9). Thompson rightly contends that Catharine "draws heavily, if erratically, from her knowledge of the Book of the Revelation" (5). As Thompson observes, Catharine's "Woe to them that shed the blood of saints," echoes "for they have shed the blood of saints" in Revelation 16:6. Catharine's "Woe, woe, woe, at the judgment" parallels the "Woe, woe, woe to the inhabiters of the earth" of Revelation 8:13. However, if Catharine's words resonate with the language of Revelation, the rest of her speech is more stylistically aligned with the short-phrase woe cries in Matthew and Luke (Matt: 23:13–16; Luke 6:24–26; Luke 11:42–47) than with the only other woe statements in Revelation, "one woe is past," "the second woe is past," "the third woe cometh" (9:12; 11:14).

The woe oracles in Isaiah 5:18–23 offer helpful background for Catharine's prophetic woe speech. Central to God's plan in Isaiah is that disorder and desolation will ravage Judah and Israel before restoration takes place. Isaiah cries out against the social and spiritual evils that he encounters in his socio-historical context. In the verses prior to this passage, the prophet cries out against land usurpation and unjust agricultural practice. Like that of Catharine's woe oracle, Isaiah's tone is bitter as he denounces those whose pride strengthens their unbelief, whose concept of justice is reversed, or whose dependence on alcohol perverts their response to righteousness:

> Woe unto them that draw iniquity with cords of vanity, and sin as it were with a cart rope: That say, Let him make speed, and hasten his work, that we may see it: and let the counsel of the Holy One of Israel draw nigh and come, that we may know it! Woe unto them that call evil good, and good evil; that put darkness for light, and light for darkness; that put bitter for sweet, and sweet for bitter! Woe unto them that are wise in their own eyes, and prudent in their own sight! Woe unto them that are mighty to drink wine, and men of strength to mingle strong drink: Which justify the wicked for reward, and take away the righteousness of the righteous from him![9] (Isaiah 5:18–23)

---

[9] For scholarly commentary on this passage, see Hans Wildberger, *Isaiah: A Continental Commentary*, translated by Thomas H. Trapp, 207-217, and Joseph Blenkinsopp, *Isaiah 1-39: A New*

Here, the prophet opens his argument with an agricultural image that would have been familiar to his readers. He compares those whose vanity necessarily brings iniquity upon them to animals roped to carts who trail carts behind them (Keil and Delitzsch 5:18). Isaiah strengthens his depiction by adding hypothetical dialogue to his analogy, suggesting the sneering, self-righteous words that such sinners might use (5:19). In their lack of faith, these sinners refuse to believe that God is at work in the world unless God shows them empirical evidence. Even worse than those without faith are those who reverse ethical standards (5:20). Again, vanity and an overblown sense of self-righteousness is inextricably linked with the perversion of moral codes (5:21). Finally, the prophet turns to the subject of alcohol, condemning those whose strength lies not in upright behavior or judgment, but

---

Translation with Introduction and Commentary, 208-215. Blenkinsopp observes that "the indictments in 5:8-24 and 10:1-4a are directed against the leadership whereas the poem about the divine anger threatens the people as a whole" (211). Catharine's woe oracle likewise attacks both the leaders and the general community of Puritans. Wildberger astutely notes that some misread Isaiah's woe oracle as narrowly focused on showing disorder and its repercussions. While Catharine is not the theologian Isaiah is, her diatribe puts her at risk of some of the same accusations: "Occasionally, some have given the impression that Isaiah is an advocate for a certain viewpoint about what constitutes order and, as such, does little more than point out the evil results which are to follow a destruction of order in the world, an order which, in and of itself, could bring about prosperity and peace. In reality, he is a theologian, passionately so, continually and singularly speaking about the obligations which Israel has toward its God" (Wildberger 217).

in getting drunk (5:22–23). Dependence upon drink rather than faith in God is another action that leads to punishment of the just and reward for the wicked. In short, Isaiah speaks of the hypocrisy and faithlessness he encounters, of the reversal of the appropriate order of things that God will condemn as part of his plan for ultimate restoration. Those who should deal out justice toward others are instead consumed with themselves. Those who merit rewards are punished. According to Isaiah, the world is turned upside down and those who continue to participate in these blasphemous, self-centered actions are setting themselves up for divine punishment, which the prophet describes in subsequent verses.[10]

In addition to the woe formula, Catharine will utter a different future-oriented prophetic expression. As she takes leave of the congregation she declares, "The day is coming, when ye shall call upon me to witness for ye to this one sin uncommitted, and I shall rise up and answer" (87). This echoes the language of tone of an oracle often translated in the King James Version as, "Behold, the days come...," which occurs frequently in the book of Jeremiah:

> Jer. 9:25 Behold, the days come, saith the LORD, that I will punish all them which are circumcised with the uncircumcised;

---

[10] We must bear in mind, however, that these are Isaiah's views and may not represent the historical state of affairs in Jerusalem. Like any literature, this passage gives us one side of the story. See Sweeney, *Isaiah 1-39*, 121–131.

Jer. 31:27 Behold, the days come, saith the LORD, that I will sow the house of Israel and the house of Judah with the seed of man, and with the seed of beast.

Jer. 31:31 Behold, the days come, saith the LORD, that I will make a new covenant with the house of Israel, and with the house of Judah...

In general, this formula communicates the judgment or restoration that God will carry out upon God's people.[11] As a typical closing remark for a biblical prophet, it further characterizes Catharine as a prophet.

According to Claus Westermann's 1960 work, *Basic Forms of Prophetic Speech*, this formula, "Behold, the days come," signifies the moment of the intervention of God in a biblical prophetic speech (174). *Basic Forms of Prophetic Speech* significantly developed the study of the genres of biblical prophecy. In this work he identifies the basic elements of various prophetic formulas. Consider this invented phrase as an example of the basic elements of this formula: "Woe to those who commit evil deeds, who murder men and abandon children. Therefore thus says the Lord, behold the days are coming when your children will rise up against you and your city shall become ruins." Westermann's categories for the prophetic judgment-speech are as follows: Introduction ("Woe"), Accusation ("to those who commit evil deeds"),

---

[11] For more on biblical time formulas see Simon De Vries, *From Old Revelation to New: A Tradition-Historical and Redaction-Critical Study of Temporal Transitions in Prophetic Prediction*, 74–85.

Development ("who murder men and abandon children"), Messenger Formula ("therefore thus says the Lord"), Intervention of God ("behold the days are coming"), Results of Intervention ("when your children will rise up against you and your city shall become ruins").[12] Westermann holds that the prophet was a messenger of God, not the mouthpiece of God; the prophet was one who conveyed a message using recognizable formulaic elements, not unlike those used by messengers who communicated between ancient near eastern rulers. *"These speeches are completely literary formations,"* Westermann emphatically asserts (172). Further discussion of the literary qualities of the prophetic speech lies beyond the scope of this text, but when we are aware of the patterns in prophetic speeches, allusions that contain similarities or aberrations come into relief.

In returning to colonial New England, we find that prophecy, while often associated with social outsiders, was prevalent. David Hall explains that the radical voice of Anne Hutchinson set the tone for the individual's right to interpret scripture:

> From Hutchinson to Keith and Rogers, these radicals relied on Scripture in defending their right to interpret God's commands. More, they drew on motifs which the orthodox themselves articulated— the expectation of the coming kingdom, the role of certain men as prophets. The social memory of the radicals was little different from the memory of the

---

[12] For definitions of these genres see Sweeney, *Isaiah 1-39* 512–547.

men who punished them; both groups cited Foxe, both were fascinated with the Book of Revelation. Crossing and recrossing a line that was difficult to fix, the radicals played on ambiguities intrinsic to the role of prophet. (Hall, *Puritans in the New World: A Critical Anthology*, 98)

Hall rightly emphasizes the centrality of ambiguity in the prophet's identity and the way he or she was viewed by the community. Moreover, Catharine fits the image of one who draws on scriptural motifs that the "orthodox" Puritans championed. She applies the motifs of sin and redemption to her cause, casting the Puritans as sinners in desperate need of redemption.

Quakers were often criticized for categorizing as sinners those who persecute religious fanatics. In this regard Anne Hutchinson also established a precedent: "In her footsteps followed other prophetlike outsiders who denounced the doctrines of the ministers and rejected their authority. A standard theme among the Quakers, who picked up where she left off, was to declare that all persecutors of the saints would suffer from God's anger" (Hall 97). Quakers were regularly stereotyped as being bent on rejecting authority. Historically speaking, this was not the primary focus of most colonial Quakers; nevertheless, they often did reject authoritative voices that they thought misrepresented the scriptures. Quakers maintained (and generally still do) that the Holy Spirit was the ultimate authority. Though the Bible was cherished, read, and preached as sacred literature, wooden scriptural readings deemed not in keeping with the direction of the Holy Spirit were openly criticized by Quakers (Abbott, 26).

While the Sprit was understood as inspiring the scriptures, it was also seen as continuing to work in the world. "Therefore, Friends have emphasized the ongoing work of revelation, rather than seeing it confined to a written text or a conciliar body; a conviction rooted in Scripture (John 14–16)" (Abbott, 26). This emphasis on continuing revelation could often lead to the ambiguity, the "crossing and recrossing a line that was difficult to fix" that Hall discusses. In contrast with a Puritan tendency to establish an authoritative interpretation of scripture, the leading of the Holy Spirit often caused Quakers to reevaluate the messages of the Bible based on their context and situation, and they called others to do the same. The founder of Quakerism, George Fox, disapproved of many of his contemporaries' static reading of scriptures: "I saw also how people read the Scriptures without a right sense of them, and without duly applying them to their own states" (Fox, *Journal of George Fox*, 31). Quakers were critical of dogmatic and impersonal uses of scripture that lacked sensitivity to the current context of the individual or community (Abbott, 27). And because Quakers understood the Holy Spirit to speak equally to men, women, and children, women were qualified religious leaders who were justified in contradicting male clergy. Using biblical prophetic language that applies to her situation, Catharine exhibits all of these basic Quaker perspectives in interrupting the worship service to critique the Puritans for their persecution of her family.

Catharine's condemnation of the Puritans is wholly justified: they have hanged her husband, banished her from the town, and in turn forced her to abandon her son, all for her Quaker belief. And though she seems the epitome of the outcast, she is not the only outsider. The primary characters are all outsiders: Tobias, the Puritan who lives on the edge of town and is further ostracized for adopting the Quaker boy, and Ilbriham himself, who is abandoned by his mother and attacked by the Puritan children. Yet, Hawthorne creates highly sympathetic depictions of both Tobias and Ilbriham; their exclusion from the community is the result of their compassionate natures. And though Catharine may arouse our pity, it is her prophetic declaration against the persecution she and her people have endured that sets her apart as the kind of outcast who challenges the community's powers of compassion; she makes them uncomfortable. Catharine's prophetic characteristics, her sackcloth and ashes, her entering into a trance state, and her woe oracle, all contribute to Hawthorne's portrait of a righteous prophet who is also a misguided fanatic.

When Catharine enters the narrative, Tobias has endured exclusion from the Puritans for adopting Ilbriham and for taking him to church. Catharine, moving to the front of the sanctuary during that same worship service, is about to beat Tobias out of his place as community outcast. Somewhat like the biblical Tamar, Catharine is responding to a perceived disorder that results in her family's violation and abuse, namely the persecution of the Quakers by the Puritans. The congregation and minister are disturbed by the strange disruption of their worship service by one who is a layperson and a woman. Moreover, the narrator's diction shows that Catharine's utterances are inappropriate for this context. After facing the congregation in silence, Catharine enters into a trance state, which the narrator describes as "her fit of inspiration" (81). As she begins to talk, Catharine does not at first make sense: "Her discourse gave evidence of an imagination hopelessly entangled with her reason" (81). Though Catharine's words gain increasing lucidity as she holds forth, that her imagination is "hopelessly entangled" with her capacity to reason foreshadows her ultimate inability to distinguish between her mind and her heart. Catharine's primary fault lies in her devotion to the cause of Quakerism over and above what should be her natural maternal devotion for her son.

Although Hawthorne's narrator retains mixed feelings about the colonial Quakers throughout the narrative, Catharine is not wholly bad. A degree of beauty and merit characterize her early utterances:

> It was a vague and incomprehensible rhapsody, which, however, seemed to spread its own atmosphere round the hearer's soul, and to move his feelings by some influence unconnected with the words. As she proceeded, beautiful but shadowy images would sometimes be seen, like bright things moving in a turbid river; or a strong and singularly shaped idea leapt forth, and seized at once on the understanding or the heart. (81)

Catharine does possess some positive power over her hearers. Her vagueness is her strength as her indistinct words creates an atmosphere that surrounds and moves the souls of those sitting in the church. There is something otherworldly at work here, though the degree to which it is a "truth," divine or otherwise, remains in question. In creating a strong but intangible impression on her audience, Catharine echoes Hawthorne's other conjure characters, such as the witch figures in "The Hollow of the Three Hills" or "Feathertop." On a basic, child-like level, Catharine has good intentions, and she is capable of creating beautiful imagery, but the narrator presents her reasoning as clouded by her personal experiences of persecution.

Hawthorne returns to the theme of slippery language throughout his works; finding the right words is never easy, and failure to do so can be detrimental. But as soon as Catharine's words begin to cohere, the self-centered focus of her project sours the initial beauty of her utterances:

> But the course of her unearthly eloquence soon led her to the persecutions of her sect, and from thence the step was short to her own peculiar sorrows. She was naturally a woman of mighty passions, and hatred and revenge now wrapped themselves in the garb of piety; the character of her speech was changed, her images became distinct though wild, and her denunciations had an almost hellish bitterness. (81)

As Catharine moves from a trance to increasing lucidity, the beauty she had created and her connection with the congregation dissolve. She becomes guilty of two faults: seeking pity and showing faulty piety. Self-righteousness, rather than the repentance that ought to mark one dressed in sackcloth and ashes, characterizes Catharine's speech here and throughout the story. Her passionate dedication to her cause is unattractive because she places it above her maternal obligations to her son. Once the hazy ambiguity gives way to distinct images, Catharine's words acquire "an almost hellish bitterness."

Perhaps one reason why Hawthorne values ambiguity in his historical narratives can be seen in this passage: It is difficult to root oneself in a history in which we can clearly discern negative or problematic elements. Casting ambiguity over a historical narrative renders it more appealing, and easier for the individual to connect with it in the way that best suits their perspective.

Catharine's prophetic utterance, like that of Isaiah cited earlier, betrays the specific concerns of her context, including similar charges of perverted ethical/religious standards. Her declarations may be more limited in scope than Isaiah's appear to be; nevertheless it should be noted that all biblical prophets speak out of their personal context and their particular experience of exploitation or suffering, hope or restoration. For the narrator, uncomfortable with Catharine's disruption of the service and the personal nature of her outcry, perhaps the biblical resonances in Catharine's speech display her hubris in thinking herself akin to a biblical prophet.[13] Yet, whatever we may say for the narrator, Catharine is a figure who has read the scriptures, and whose language and mission echo that of a prophet.

---

[13] Biographically speaking, a tension exists between Hawthorne's own wary view of Christianity and his appreciation for the authoritative power of biblical allusions. "The Bible had for Nathaniel Hawthorne the authority of narrative. It was a book of tales that had power outside of theology and history—close to myth—that is, close to psychological and ethical truth because it shows action and reaction among individuals" (Robert Hudspeth 30 September 2009).

In Catharine's passionate speech to the startled Puritan congregation, we find her now beginning to confront her hearers with the full, angry force of her message. Her prophetic utterance has shifted from its indistinct quality of beauty to outcries that reflect her personal experience of oppression:

> "The Governor and his mighty men," she said, "have gathered together, taking counsel among themselves and saying, 'What shall we do unto this people—even unto the people that have come into this land to put our iniquity to the blush?' And lo! the devil entereth into the council-chamber, like a lame man of low stature and gravely appareled, with a dark and twisted countenance, and a bright, downcast eye. And he standeth up among the rulers; yea, he goeth to and fro, whispering to each; and every man lends his ear, for his word is 'slay, slay!'" (81-82)

As in Isaiah's prophetic oracle, Catharine begins by describing those who are participating in evil actions: "The Governor and his mighty men." Her sarcastic use of the adjective, "mighty," when it becomes clear that they are only mighty in performing evil acts, belies Catharine's bitterness as she starts her tirade. She continues in the biblical prophetic style by proposing what these individuals might be saying when they assemble: "What shall we do unto this people—even unto this people that put our iniquity to the blush?" The words Catharine puts into the mouths of the Puritans she condemns depict them as aware of their sinful behavior and eager to persecute those who would uncover their inequity. Catharine then reveals the source of their evil, the devil himself, who, disguised as a lame man, slips in among the governor's men. The men seem to listen eagerly to the evil commandments of the devil: "slay, slay!" With this introduction, Catharine has established the reversal of justice she believes to be at work in the Puritan government: they who claim to act for the cause of righteousness seek to destroy the true bearers of the light, the Quakers, who in turn know the Puritan government's sinister nature. Moreover, the Puritan authorities are informed and inspired by the devil and readily deal out vengeance at his suggestion. By giving voice to the unrighteous, she, like Isaiah, seeks to strengthen her case against them.

As in the Isaiah passage discussed, the series of woe oracles that follow Catharine's introduction enable her to highlight the evils of the Puritans more specifically. Catharine's use of this mode carries her from the generally murderous acts of the Puritans to the particulars of her own experience of persecution, and ultimately to the judgment that will come to those who kill:

> But I say unto ye, Woe to them that slay! Woe to them that shed the blood of saints! Woe to them that have slain the husband, and cast forth the child, the tender infant, to wander homeless, and hungry, and cold, till he die; and have saved the mother alive, in the cruelty of their tender mercies! Woe to them that shed the blood of saints! Woe to them in their life-time, cursed are they in the delight and pleasure of their hearts! Woe to them in their death hour, whether it come swiftly with blood and violence, or after long and lingering pain! Woe, in the dark house, in the rottenness of the

grave, when the children's children shall revile the ashes of the fathers! Woe, woe, woe, at the judgment, when all the persecuted and all the slain in this bloody land, and the father, the mother, and the child, shall await them in a day that they cannot escape! (82)

Catharine's use of the exclamation, *woe*, like Isaiah's, serves as a warning. Before prophesying that the innocent slain will meet their persecutors on the judgment day, she condemns those responsible for her current predicament: her husband was killed, her son abandoned, and she has been banished by the Puritans. Catharine's wish for her persecutors to suffer is not uncommon among the voices of the Hebrew Bible, but the narrator characterizes her as just as bitter and bloodthirsty as those she cries out against. Repetition adds fire to her rampage, as when she repeats the line, "Woe to them that shed the blood of saints!" and in the penultimate line, "Woe, woe, woe at the judgment..."[14] Rather than offering a vision of God judging the sinners on the judgment day, Catharine envisions people like herself and her murdered husband, "all the persecuted and all the slain," casting judgment upon those who hurt them. It is in this vision that she truly exposes her self-focused agenda. God should be the judge on the judgment day, not Catharine. The narrator sees

---

[14] C.f. Revelation 8:13: "Woe, woe, woe to the inhabiters of the earth." Additionally, Catharine's words, "Woe to them that shed the blood of saints" echo those of Revelation 16:6: "For they have shed the blood of saints and prophets, and thou hast given them blood to drink; for they are worthy." Maule's curse in *Seven Gables* also alludes to this line from Revelation.

the same goodness and beauty in the innocent, original concept of Quakerism that we find in the positive depictions of little Ilbrahim and mentions of the inner light throughout the narrative. But Catharine's prophetic rant reflects how destructive anger becomes to an originally beautiful concept.

At the end of her speech, Catharine calls the Puritan congregation to repent, reflecting another theme central to prophetic literature. She also urges them to proclaim judgment against those among them who are guilty of persecution:

> Seed of the faith, seed of the faith,[15] ye whose hearts
> are moving with a power that ye know not, arise,

---

[15] The expression, "seed of the faith" is not strictly scriptural. It may be connected to the phrase, "seed of Israel" that appears in several Hebrew Bible texts such as Isaiah 6:13 and Ezra 9 and refers to Israel/Judah. In religious documents contemporary to colonial Puritanism, "seed of faith" generally implies "righteous Christians," as opposed to the "seed of Cain" who are the evil descendants of the first person to commit murder and as such are aligned with the devil. (See Laurence Claxton, *Look about you For the Devil that you fear is in you: OR, THE RIGHT DEVIL UN-FOLDED* (London: William Learner, 1659) A3: "To you the Seed of Faith, the only beloved Family of the Lord of Glory, your poor despised Brother, yet heir with you of that immortal endless kingdom, saluteth you as followeth: In this Treatise I have brought to publique view your grand Opposite *Cain*, the father of al the devils children...") "Seed of the faith" can also imply a sense of the original seed or pure minority of a religion amid a sinful majority. When the expression, "Seed of Israel" is paired with the phrase "Seed of Jacob" in the Hebrew Bible, the way in which the referents are understood as the people of God relates to the histor-

wash your hands of this innocent blood! Lift your
voices, chosen ones, cry aloud, and call down a woe
and a judgment with me! (82)

These closing lines of Catharine's declaration fall under the
biblical scholarly category of *prophetic exhortation*. A common
prophetic form, the prophetic exhortation encourages hearers
to act (Sweeney, *The Prophetic Literature* 41). This form is
frequently pared with an admonition, such as the woe oracle,
"which attempts to persuade against a particular course of
action. Together, the two forms constitute a paranesis, which
is an address to an individual or group that attempts to persuade with reference to a goal" (Sweeney, *The Prophetic Literature*, 42).[16] Catharine's address to the Puritan congregation uses these two commonly paired prophetic formulas. As
is also the case with this pairing of prophetic formulas, a call
to repentance is tied up with the exhortation. As Sweeney
explains, the prophetic exhortation "is generally associated
with the motif of repentance. It makes little sense to maintain that the prophets simply announced judgment without
attempting to influence their addressees. Otherwise, they
had little reason to speak" (42). Hawthorne recognized and
used such basic prophetic formulas in his characterization of
Catharine. She is keenly concerned with influencing her au-

---

ical narratives of the ancestral covenants made with God. (E.g.
Psalm 22:23: "Ye that fear the LORD, praise him; all ye the seed
of Jacob, glorify him; and fear him, all ye the seed of Israel.") The
sense of a nation founded on a divine covenant, as is the case with
Israel in the Hebrew Bible, echoes the idea of America's founded
as a divinely sanctioned enterprise.

[16] See also Sweeney, *Isaiah 1-39*, 520.

dience. She has no qualms about risking her social standing, her life, and even that of her child, to persuade the Puritans: she urges them to fear the judgment that their sect's violence will bring about, to repent, and to condemn those among them who persecute the Quakers.

Following Catharine's speech, the narrator is quick to disapprove of her ecstatic declarations: "Having thus given vent to the flood of malignity which she mistook for inspiration, the speaker was silent" (82). While there may have been some transient value in Catharine's early and indistinct utterances, much of her speech jars the audience. And for our narrator, there is no affirming quality of influence in an utterance driven by malignity, at least not for a woman speaking thus out of turn in such a context. Of course, the narrator may not necessarily be a reliable guide, but his perspective naturally influences our reaction to the characters. Catharine's outburst will contrast with the tender moment she shares with her son, a contrast that will highlight her inability to be both prophet and mother.

The audience is indeed uncomfortable with Catharine's prophecy. The stereotype of the biblical prophet is of one whose message goes unheeded by the masses. Indeed, the prophetic literature often describes a prophet's frustration with the lack of communal adherence to his prophecies. This narrative depiction should remain distinct from historical understanding, however. "Many scholars uncritically presume that Israel rejected the message of the prophets and therefore were punished, but the fact of the matter is that we have no idea how the people reacted to them. The fact that the prophetic books were included in the Bible suggests that someone took them quite seriously" (Sweeney 6 August

2009). Yet in "The Gentle Boy," Catharine embodies the stereotype of the unheeded, even despised, prophet. Several women are greatly upset by the incident, crying out in "hysteric shrieks" (82) following Catharine's speech. The rest of the congregation are struck dumb: "They remained stupefied, stranded as it were, in the midst of a torrent, which deafened them by its roaring, but might not move them by its violence" (82). Later, Catharine's brief expression of maternal tenderness will open their hearts, but the violent mode of her outcry prevents her hearers from being stirred to accept or even consider her perspective.

Catharine embodies significant qualities of biblical prophets, but she is not met with the reception of one who brings an authoritative or divine message, as does the Gray Champion. How is Hawthorne using prophecy here and what thematic results come from it? Hawthorne presents several typical characteristics of a biblical prophet, which creates a stereotypical prophetic figure. He also shows that there exist tensions between fanaticism and oppression. That Catharine cries out against the persecution of the Quakers is reasonable. That she is upset about her husband's murder is appropriate. That she interrupts a worship service with wild and violent language is where she begins to err. And yet, in so doing she is still in line with what a biblical prophet might do, crying out against injustices, often amid perceived hypocrites, at a time and place when no one wants to hear it. Where she essentially differs from the prophets is in casting herself as a judge at the end time. She may indeed be confused on this point, but we must recall that this is an oppressed woman: her husband has just been hanged and she has been separated from her son through her banishment.

Hawthorne holds the larger thematic concepts of fanaticism and oppression together and tests the ways in which they conflict, the fashion by which one draws the other out. Oppression prompts fanatic behavior. Fanatic behavior leads to oppression.

At the minister's command that Catharine step down from the pulpit and cease "to pour fourth the foulness of [her] heart, and the inspiration of the devil" (83), Catharine acquiesces. Her response embodies both the Quaker notion that the divine Spirit spoke through the individual, and the concept that the prophet is the mouthpiece of God through whom the deity communicates to the people: "'I go, friend, I go, for the voice hath had its utterance,' replied she, in a depressed and even mild tone. 'I have done my mission unto thee and to thy people. Reward me with stripes, imprisonment, or death, as ye shall be permitted'" (83). During her trance state, Catharine was under the influence of an outside entity of some sort. She believes it was the voice of truth; the minister maintains that it was the devil. The notion of the divine Spirit speaking through an individual is central to Quakerism (and heretical from a Puritan perspective). Of course, this is central to biblical prophecy as well. The prophets aren't God, but they are the vessels through whom God speaks.

A question of authority is at issue here. Biblical writers themselves were not in the practice of questioning the authority of the prophets they depicted as communicating on behalf of God. Yet we do question Catharine's authority. In biblical prophetic literature, prophetic utterances are characterized as authoritative and are generally intended to be viewed in a positive light. Hawthorne, on the other hand, constantly questions such claims of authority in his text. He does not characterize Catharine's utterances as wholly authoritative, nor does he cast them in a positive light. In her lack of compassion for the people to whom she prophesies, she is ultimately unable to convert them to her perspective. Though her actions on behalf of an oppressed people align with those of biblical prophets, the negative way Hawthorne portrays her lessens her authority. Still, Catharine's determination to carry out her mission to the Puritan people reflects the basic office of the biblical prophet. Though she is hardly a reluctant prophet, in some ways we might compare her prophesying against a people not her own, the Puritans, to Jonah's prophesying against the Ninevites who would persecute his own people. Not unlike Catharine, Jonah himself is not depicted favorably, but his prophecies are justified in their call for repentance.

Catharine is positively characterized when she succumbs to a moment of maternal tenderness. When little Ilbrahim emerges from the crowd and calls out to her she sobs, "My heart was withered; yea, dead with thee and with thy father; and now it leaps as in the first moment when I pressed thee to my bosom" (84). While in the arms of her son, Catharine appreciates that her heart had not been alive since her husband and son were taken from her; now she feels it jolting to life in the presence of her offspring. It is at this moment that Catharine can once again create something beautiful. She affects the congregation not by any conscious or even semiconscious effort to persuade them, but, as in her indistinct words before her woe oracle, through emotional, non-verbal utterances: "the joy that could find no words, expressed itself in broken accents, like bubbles gushing up to vanish at the surface of a deep fountain" (84). The narrator seems to suggest that Catharine should give in to her woman's instincts and let go of her sense of religious calling. Whenever she takes up her cause she sows discord around her, and bitterness in her own heart. Yet the narrator states that Catharine's spell of joyful tenderness is fleeting:

> Soon, however, the spectators saw a change upon her face, as the consciousness of her sad estate returned, and grief supplied the fount of tears which joy had opened. By the words she uttered, it would seem that the indulgence of natural love had given her mind a momentary sense of its errors, and made her know how far she had strayed from duty, in following the dictates of a wild fanaticism. (84)

Once Catharine's analytical mind grows cognizant of having yielded to maternal affection, she composes herself and once again allows her personal sorrows to feed her tears, rather than to let them fall from the joy of seeing her son.

Catharine's prophetic characteristics, her sackcloth and ashes, her entering into a trance state, her woe oracle, all contribute to Hawthorne's portrait of a righteous prophet and a misguided fanatic. She resembles a prophet in many ways, but her fanaticism undercuts her ability to be a mother. On an important level she is in the right: the Puritans have sinned as a community by persecuting the Quakers. And in the fleeting moment when her fanaticism gives way to compassion, she positively influences those around her. When Catharine is not forming actual sentences or following any logical train of thought, as in the early moments of her prophetic utterance or in her emotional state when she beholds her son, she lets down her guard and both embodies and creates something beautiful and pure. As she resumes her composure and becomes the cold fanatic once again, she stands in stark contrast with Dorothy, the loving Puritan woman who wants to look after Ilbrahim: "The two females, as they held each a hand of Ilbrahim, formed a practical allegory; it was rational piety and unbridled fanaticism, contending for the empire of a young heart" (85). The brief moments of tenderness show us that Catharine is capable of thoughtful, maternal tenderness, but as her feeling of obligation to her people informs her sense of self, she will remain the polar opposite of rational piety: "unbridled fanaticism."

Catharine seals her position as more prophet than mother by leaving her son with Dorothy and uttering a future-oriented prophetic formula: "The day is coming, when ye shall call upon me to witness for ye to this one sin uncommitted, and I shall rise up and answer" (87). When such expressions occur in biblical prophetic literature, they usually represent the words of God, spoken through the prophet. As cited earlier, this formula occurs frequently in the book of Jeremiah. Characteristic of the Quaker tendency to apply scripture to one's personal concerns and circumstances, Catharine manipulates this formula for her purposes at the end of the church scene.

Of course, we do not know if Hawthorne specifically intended to link Catharine's words with generic prophetic speech formulas. But our understanding of the prophets enriches our understanding of what Hawthorne wrote. There is enough similarity between her words and recognizable prophetic elements that a few distinctions appear significant. Perhaps the primary difference is Catharine's casting herself, rather than God, as the one who will judge the deeds of the Puritans. Judgment is the purview of God according to the prophetic literature. In abandoning her child to prophesy in ashes and sackcloth for the Quaker cause, Catharine is already worthy of censure according to the narrator and the Puritan community. But in appropriating the role of cosmic judge over the sinners at the end time, she is operating out of a distorted psychological and moral reality. True, it is the prophet's purview to alert the public to injustices that are being carried out. As such, Catharine's cry to have the Puritan congregation "call down a judgment" with her stands within the appropriate limits of the office of the prophet. But to declare that "The day is coming, when ye shall call upon me to witness for ye to this one sin uncommitted, and I shall rise up and answer," (87) Catharine blurs the line between fighting justice in the world of the living and serving a divine role on the judgment day. This exposes a flaw in the nature of prophecy as Catharine represents it.

A further question should be explored regarding Catharine's closing line: what does this strange declaration even mean? Her use of the odd phrase, "sin uncommitted," recalls the narrator's description of her as one in possession of "an imagination hopelessly entangled with her reason." Is Catharine referring to the good deed of Dorothy and Tobias, that Ilbrahim is not dead after all—as she seems heretofore to have assumed—because he was saved from death by their adopting him? Is she declaring that she will advocate for the couple that lovingly adopted her son? If so, the prophetic tones of the opening and closing phrases of this sentence suggest that she will be called upon "to witness" in another physical reality. Even if she is not alluding to an after-life, this manner of foreknowledge is generally attributed to God speaking *through* a prophet. Still, her declaration is unclear: who exactly will call upon her to witness for them? What is the "one sin uncommitted"? What does she mean by "rise up"? What will this "answer" be? The ambiguity of the line ultimately resists conclusive analysis. Hawthorne's own reservations about the technical merits of his short story might also caution us not to take our reading too far. It is neither a biblical quotation nor a sentence in the spirit of the prophetic literature; it is a skewed, ambiguous rendering of a prophetic declaration reflecting both the conflicted character of Catharine and Hawthorne's tendency to imbue his historical narratives with a degree of ambiguity and irony. Perhaps Hawthorne himself is the persecutor: he makes us witness to the conflicts between fanaticism and oppression played out in a moral tragedy the Puritans and Quakers could not fully comprehend.

Despite her misguided declarations, Catharine's plight, in necessary conjunction with her tender exchange with her son, ultimately stirs the compassion of the congregation. As Catharine leaves, "a general sentiment of pity overcame the virulence of religious hatred. Sanctified by her love, and her affliction, she went forth, and all the people gazed after her till she had journeyed up the hill, and was lost behind its brow. She went, the apostle of her own unquiet heart, to renew the wanderings of past years" (87). These tender lines illustrate that Catharine gains the sympathy not only of the congregation, but also of the narrator. Though her reasoning may be confused, "her love, and her affliction" allow her some sanctification in the eyes of the narrator, and perhaps the congregation as well. Once Catharine displays her capacity for compassion, the narrator's diction reflects his own compassion for her. Drawing the scene to a close with such words as, "she went, the apostle of her own unquiet heart," the narrator has come to view Catharine with a pity beyond that which the congregation is able to show. The Pearsons and Ilbrahim, none of whom enjoy full membership in either the Quaker or Puritan communities, are the only characters who are capable of genuine pity.[17]

The storyteller has presented a whirlwind of conflicting feelings by this point in the narrative: we have been lured toward sympathy for the Quakers by the image of the innocent, abandoned Ilbrahim. We've witnessed the compassion of the Puritans in the kindness of Dorothy and Tobias. Now the narrator turns to Islam and describes the Muslims as having been more compassionate than either the Quakers or the Puritans: "Her mission had extended also to the followers of the Prophet, and from them she had received the courtesy and kindness, which all the contending sects of our purer religion united to deny her" (88). We further learn that Ilbrahim was born in Turkey and that his "oriental name"

---

[17] Pity prompts Tobias to rescue the boy, and perhaps pity ultimately defeats Tobias. Just as he is situated somewhere in between the Puritan and the Quaker communities, Tobias' name alludes neither to the Protestant Old Testament nor the New Testament, but rather to the Apocrypha. W. R. Thompson notes "the parallel situations of Tobit, father of the Apocryphal Tobias, and Tobias Pearson. Tobit befriended those who were persecuted by the temporal powers of Nineveh. For his pains he was deprived of his possessions, driven out, and threatened with death" (n. 10).

was chosen because of the kindnesses of the Muslims and the Sultan: "the good deeds of an unbeliever" (87). After describing the faults and merits of the Quakers and Puritans, the narrator further complicates the picture by depicting Islam in a positive, ironic, light. The Christian denominations are presented as neither wholly bad nor wholly good, and the Muslims are romanticized and exoticized. These competing views of different religious traditions, in conjunction with Catharine's taking on the character of fanatic prophet, work together to cast a characteristic Hawthornian irony over this early colonial period. Just as ambiguity protects the narrative from conclusive interpretation, irony serves as protection against fanaticism.

Catharine is not present in the second part of the narrative, which depicts Ilbrahim befriending and then being beaten by the Puritan boy and his playmates. However, the closing line of the middle section of the story depicts Catharine's continuing plight: "to wander on a mistaken errand, neglectful of the holiest trust which can be committed to a woman" (95). Whatever the compassion bestowed upon the prophetess by community or narrator, in living for her Quaker cause rather than her son, she remains a long-suffering individual, her prophetic guise and posture rendering her tragic and finally incapable of bringing about genuine restoration.

Catharine then returns in the final section of the story. Tobias has converted to Quakerism but is losing his faith as the gentle boy lingers near death, never having recovered emotionally from the attack of the "baby fiends," the Puritan children. Catharine bursts upon the bleak winter scene with biblical language denoting affirmation and restoration, rather than the ill-portending prophecy of her earlier utterances: "'Rejoice, friends!' she replied. 'Thou who hast long been of our people, and thou whom a little child hath led to us, rejoice! Lo! I come, the messenger of glad tidings, for the day of persecution is overpast. The heart of the king, even Charles, hath been moved in gentleness towards us" (101). Catharine's joyful declaration regarding King Charles' pronouncement that it is unlawful to persecute Quakers alludes to the vision of the peaceable kingdom in Isaiah 11:1–9: "The wolf also shall dwell with the lamb, and the leopard shall lie down with the kid; and the calf and the young lion and the fatling together; and a little child shall lead them" (11:6). Isaiah's depiction of nonviolence among God's creation is part of a vision of the peace that will come with a righteous ruler, "the stem of Jesse" (11:1aβ). Not surprisingly, however, Catharine's prophetic allusion houses the image in a rather different context, insofar as her reference to the little child pertains to the boy who led Tobias to Quakerism. In contrast, the biblical passage refers to the child leading the animals, wild and gentle alike, in a foreshadowed time of peace under a righteous ruler. It seems here that the reference is not meant to add scriptural support to the character's endeavors, but to debunk her endeavors because of her manipulation of the biblical text.[18]

---

[18] Neither does Catharine refer to the remainder of the passage, Isaiah 11:10–16, which describes the future restoration of Israel and the return of the exiles from other nations. Perhaps Catharine's omission of the return of the exiles is significant insofar as her perception of her people as outsiders is too closely

But now Catharine is positively depicted, having become a compassionate mother once more. After arriving at the house primarily to seek out her son, she grows frantic at the thought of his lingering near death: "she shook like a leaf, she turned white as the very snow that hung drifted into her hair" (101). Catharine goes through several phases from this point to the end of the tale. At her first understanding of Ilbrahim's predicament she is faint, speaking in a whisper. Then she enters a passionate state: she "broke forth with sudden and irrepressible violence" (102). Catharine's fervor is heightened by its contrast with the hushed house she enters upon. Though the old Quaker man speaks of Ilbrahim as if he is already dead, we discover that the boy has not yet departed, and "when Catharine's shriek pierced through the room, the boy strove to raise himself" (102). When her passion rages for the sake of her dying son, Catharine's fury is jarring, but appropriate. This is where the narrator would have preferred her violent passions to have focused, rather than in her sense of her prophetic mission.

Though Catherine comes to her son because King Charles has banned the persecution of Quakers, she stands devastated at the prospect of her dying Ilbrahim: "I am a woman, I am but a woman" whispers Catharine at the opening of her response to the Quaker man. By the end of her speech her whisper has swelled to an outcry. Catharine's raised voice shows the full degree to which her passions have shifted to the cause of her son rather than the cause of her

---

aligned with her mission as a Quaker for her understanding of restoration to involve an end to the exilic status of her people.

sect: "Give me back the boy, well, sound, alive, alive; or earth and heaven shall avenge me!" (102). With a powerful, poetic quality that echoes Catharine's earlier prophetic utterance, her explosion is that of a desperate mother, not a desperate prophet. These are Catharine's last words in the narrative, the final lines of speech being given to her son, who is and ever was, the purer example of pity and compassion.

Though Catharine's maternal attachment to her son— and the victory for the Quakers—temporarily overshadows her prophetic mission, she is ultimately unable to mother him while he is alive and well. In a reversal of the usual parent-to-child flow of compassion, Catharine looks upon her son in agony while Ilbrahim's last words console his despairing mother: "'Mourn not, dearest mother. I am happy now.' And with these words, the gentle boy was dead" (104). Whether or not it is a manifestation of mourning, Catharine's fervor only grows stronger at the death of the last of her kin, surpassing her former fervor: "Catharine's fanaticism had become wilder by the sundering of all human ties" (104). But by the story's end, Catharine comes to be pitied by the Puritans. It is telling that once their behavior softens and becomes charitable, her demeanor softens as well. This suggests that her prophetic fanaticism was largely a reaction to communal abuse, reinforcing the probability that her actions were those of a woman in pain rather than the actions of a "real" prophet. As the circle of compassion expands within the community, the now yielding Catharine comes to live out the rest of her life in the Pearson home. There the sweet spirit of her departed Ilbrahim continues her education in compassion, "as if his gentle spirit came down from heaven to teach his parent a true religion, her fierce and vindictive nature was softened by the same griefs which had once irritated it" (104). Catharine is softened by the spirit of mercy and goodness that the gentle boy exudes before and after death. The political victory of the Quakers, the tenderness of the gradually mellowing Puritan community around her, and the presence of her son's gentle spirit, finally quiet her fiery nature.

As it never is in Hawthorne's stories, "The Gentle Boy" is not a clear-cut narrative from America's past of good versus bad, of stereotypically dour Puritans seeking to eradicate the nonviolent Quakers or even of noble Puritans rightly condemning radical Quakers. Hawthorne's plot turns and elements of irony remind us not to trust in simplistic interpretations of history. That Catharine's heart was too bent on championing the Quaker cause to leave room to love her son shows the reader that the nonviolent Quakers are fallible. That the Puritans would leave a small child to die in the wilderness shows the risks inherent in the extreme tendencies of that denomination.

In the biblical tradition, prophets arise out of times of transition, persecution, or the chaos of national formation. The prophets "were essentially concerned with the problem of evil, whether of divine or human origin, in their own day" (Sweeney, *The Prophetic Literature*, 217). Catharine as prophet is likewise concerned with the problem of evil in her own day. Yet Catharine's fanaticism disables her ability to act out of compassion, which makes her unable either to serve as mother or to truly convert the hearts of the people to whom she prophesies. Hawthorne thus reveals his skepticism of contemporary prophecy. And in exposing the faults of both the Quakers and the Puritans, Hawthorne explores the tensions between fanaticism and oppression. Catharine's fanaticism grows out of her experience of violent oppression. Oppression prompts fanaticism, and vice versa. As the story draws to a close, both lessen in tandem. Biblical prophets likewise respond to oppression with what may be considered fanatic behavior. But Hawthorne's prophets must respond with love as well as fire to evince constructive transformation. It may be that in his use of the woe formula and other prophetic elements, Hawthorne is creating a passage with biblical overtones to lend the scene a mythic quality, or, in his quest to create a distinctly American history, simply the sense of a story that took place long ago. Whatever the reason, Catharine's fiery character shows that prophetic elements shape Hawthorne's concern with creating a nuanced American literary history, one in which even would-be prophets play a part in the origins of the nation.

3

Parable, Prophecy, and Symbolic Action in

"The Minister's Black Veil"

Hawthorne places "The Minister's Black Veil" in two generic categories: parable and twice-told tale. On a surface level, "twice-told" identifies Hawthorne's tales that were published in a magazine before appearing in a book. However, this descriptor bears multiple meanings. In his study on literary allegory, Edwin Honing defines the term as follows:

> "Twice-told" means that a venerated or proverbial (old) story has become the pattern for a new one. The new story—the allegory—uses figurative language in order that the old and new can be told simultaneously, and the belief expressed is the reason for the retelling. This means that an image or a detail in an allegory is not of importance primarily in itself nor for the story but as an instance or illustration of something in the old story, in the meaning or referent. The allegorist does not begin with an image which suggests a meaning, but he begins with an idea or meaning and looks for an image to

represent it. (Honing, *Dark Conceit: The Making of Allegory*, 5)

Here, Honing suggests that twice-told tales are allegories. The degree to which we can read each of Hawthorne's twice-told tales as allegorical may vary, though such an approach would yield provocative results. Indeed, in "The Minister's Black Veil" we find an "old story"—venerated for its setting in colonial New England—that "has become the pattern for a new one" written in the nineteenth century. Historical tales are Hawthorne's way of addressing questions or issues of his time, or of all times. The "idea or meaning" central to this twice-told tale is the power of mystery represented by the black veil.

Hawthorne's narrator communicates the veil's powerful effect upon the community through the opening lines of the story that describe the *impact* of the veil, rather than the veil itself. Moreover, the first words about the veil are those of the sexton's reaction to it, not of an omniscient narrator:

> THE sexton stood in the porch of Milford meeting-house, pulling busily at the bell-rope. The old people of the village came stooping along the street. Children, with bright faces, tripped merrily beside their parents, or mimicked a graver gait, in the conscious dignity of their Sunday clothes. Spruce bachelors looked sidelong at the pretty maidens, and fancied that the Sabbath sunshine made them prettier than on week days. When the throng had mostly streamed into the porch, the sexton began to toll the bell, keeping his eye on the Reverend Mr. Hooper's door. The first glimpse of the clergyman's

figure was the signal for the bell to cease its summons.

"But what has good Parson Hooper got upon his face?" cried the sexton in astonishment. All within hearing immediately turned about, and beheld the semblance of Mr. Hooper, pacing slowly his meditative way towards the meeting-house. With one accord they started, expressing more wonder than if some strange minister were coming to dust the cushions of Mr. Hooper's pulpit. (37–38)

In these few lines, the narrator shows the veil's interruption of the pleasant Sunday morning scene. The sexton speaks that which the reader wonders: What manner of thing is on Hooper's face? Neither is the reader's curiosity satisfied when, a few lines later, Hawthorne presents a more unsettling mystery:

Swathed about his forehead, and hanging down over his face, so low as to be shaken by his breath, Mr. Hooper had on a black veil. On a nearer view it seemed to consist of two folds of crape, which entirely concealed his features, except the mouth and chin, but probably did not intercept his sight, further than to give a darkened aspect to all living and inanimate things. (38)

The minister's black veil will cloud the view of everyone involved in the story, including the reader. So begins a narrative about a prophet whose calling involves coming into proximity with mystery. Like other of Hawthorne's prophets, Hooper understands pain (as does Catharine) and treats the community with compassion (as Catharine does not). The religious lives of some are deepened by Hooper's action. But others are put off by it and do not undergo transformation. The responsibility for growth lies in the parishioners' manner of responding to mystery.

Hooper's veil bears a resemblance to the veil worn by Moses after his encounters with the divine in Exodus 34. Exodus 34:29–35 serves as a conclusion to the golden calf narrative begun in Exodus 32: though the narrator deems the people to have sinned in worshiping the golden calf, they have now achieved a restoration through Moses' work as a mediator between God and the people.

> And it came to pass, when Moses came down from mount Sinai with the two tables of testimony in Moses' hand, when he came down from the mount, that Moses wist not that the skin of his face shone while he talked with him. And when Aaron and all the children of Israel saw Moses, behold, the skin of his face shone; and they were afraid to come nigh him. And Moses called unto them; and Aaron and all the rulers of the congregation returned unto him: and Moses talked with them. And afterward all the children of Israel came nigh: and he gave them in commandment all that the LORD had spoken with him in mount Sinai. And till Moses had done speaking with them, he put a vail on his face. But when Moses went in before the LORD to speak with him, he took the vail off, until he came out. And he came out, and spake unto the children of Israel that which he was commanded. And the children of Israel saw the face of Moses, that the skin of Moses' face shone: and Moses put the vail upon his

face again, until he went in to speak with him. (Exodus 34:29–35)

Upon his return from talking with God in the mountain, Moses' glowing face alarms the people to the point that they run away in fear. Moses calls first to Aaron and the religious leaders and talks to them. Only after they confer with Moses do the people venture to approach him, perhaps understanding through the leaders that it is safe to be in the presence of Moses. When he first returns from the mountain, Moses is unaware that he has undergone any physical transformation. Perhaps after he has come to understand the horror the change in his face strikes in the people, or maybe due to the inappropriateness of continuing to show his face after this encounter with God, Moses begins to cover his face with a veil. But the veil is always removed when he talks to God or when he relates God's words to the people. As the passage ends, it can be assumed that, excepting the times when he is interacting with the divine or mediating between God and the people, Moses wears the veil for the rest of his life (Propp, *Exodus 19–40: A New Translation with Introduction and Commentary*, 618).

Biblical scholars offer several possible explanations of this account. The veil may be a feature of an oracular prophet (Sweeney, 10 December 2009). In the context of the ancient Israelite temple, the veil may have represented a covering of the Holy of Holies that separates the ark from the rest of the sanctuary. As such, it represents a sacred boundary between figures that interact with God (Sweeney, 10 December 2009). The veil covers up that which human eyes are unworthy to view, and or the experience of which is overwhelming to mortals. The Hebrew term, קָרַן (*qaran*), generally translated with the prophet's name as "Moses' face shone," could also be rendered, "his skin was *toughened*" or "his forehead sprouted *horns*" (Propp, 620). While there is evidence that "horns were a sign of divinity in the ancient Near East," it is impossible to draw conclusions about what Moses' transformed face is meant to have looked like (Propp, 623). William Propp states that the face of Moses, "branded by Yahweh—whether horned, beaming or hardened—becomes the Mask of God" (623). This is particularly significant in that the face of God often functions as "a hypostasis, i.e., a part of the divine being that stands for the whole" (Propp, 619). The face of the human being who directly encounters God becomes, in this narrative, no longer viewable by human eyes. Still, as Brevard Childs argues, "Moses' face should not be understood as a type of metamorphosis. Moses did not himself become a deity. He was unaware of any transformation. The whole point of the story emphasizes that his was only a reflection of God's glory" (Childs, *The Book of Exodus: A Critical, Theological Commentary*, 619). Moses is merely the mediator, but he mediates for God, and his office is such that his face must henceforth always remain veiled when he is not speaking with or for the Deity.

What can be the implications of this for "The Minister's Black Veil"? If Reverend Hooper is aligned with Moses in the Exodus narrative, it could be said that Hooper has an encounter with God before he emerges, veiled, for Sunday service. It could also be said, then, that he has no further direct contact with God, if he indeed had any in the first place. Furthermore, as Moses' face remains unveiled when he communicates God's words to the people, the fact that Hooper's remains veiled for the rest of his life would suggest that he has no words of God to offer the people either. In this sense he does not function as a mediatory between the divine and humanity. Or if he does, he is a frustrated, hybrid mediator, having had the transformative encounter with God that led him to don the veil, but not the ability to fulfill the transaction by offering new messages to the people. It is also possible that the failure of communication lies with the people, rather than Hooper, and that they are unable to perceive a direct message from God.

Hooper's veil thus seems to serve the opposite function of Moses' veil: whereas Moses' veil hides his terrifying face from the people, Hooper's *veil* is what terrifies the people. Had they seen his face in some awful, transformed state before he began to wear it, the veil would have taken on an entirely different meaning for them: it would have buffered them from something frightening or that they were not worthy to behold. But they are left to speculate as to what the veil is hiding, a prospect that disturbs them because it is unknown. The mystery of the veil, prompting people to sense that it enables Hooper to perceive their secret sins, inspires terror in the people of Hawthorne's story.

While Moses' veil and Hooper's veil are linked with both God and terror, Hooper's actions may more closely resemble the Hebrew Bible prophet carrying out a strange symbolic action, such as when Isaiah walks naked (Isaiah 20:3) or Ezekiel eats the temple scroll (Ezekiel 3:1–3). Such actions elicit numerous interpretations. Likewise, the literary critical interpretations made of Hooper's veil span from rendering Hooper as Christ to Hooper as Antichrist.[1] The mystery at the center of the story invites speculation about the implications of the veil, but the narrative's emphasis on the unknown should give us pause before ascribing specific connotations to the minister's actions. The very power of the veil derives from its terrifying quality of obscurity. In offering the reader no direct explanation of the veil, no exchange between the minister and God say, Hawthorne writes a version of a prophetic story in which crucial information is left out. As a result, the narrative pushes the notion of mystery to an unsatisfying end: perhaps the strange symbolic action of donning the veil suggests that the unknowability of the world, of the human heart, is something with which every individual must live.

Contemplating Hooper's wearing of the veil as a prophetic, symbolic action offers several helpful categories for analyzing "The Minister's Black Veil." These categories provide ways to discuss Hooper's mysterious undertaking, especially since the symbolic action narrative is a genre suited to mystery. A just account of this literature must allow for the obscurity inherent in the very notion of the symbolic action. This approach emphasizes the veil's power of mysterious obscurity, and the centrality of retaining the mystery, rather than forcing an interpretation, of the minister's black veil.

Critics have been exploring biblical themes in Hawthorne's "The Minister's Black Veil" for decades. Gilbert P. Voight proposed a parallel between Hooper's veil and the

---

[1] See Judy McCarthy, "'The Minister's Black Veil': Concealing Moses and the Holy of Holies," and William Bysshe Stein, *Hawthorne's Faust: A Study of the Devil Archetype.*

symbolic actions of the biblical prophets in 1952: "Perhaps the godly preacher is simply resorting to the ancient Hebrew prophets' practice of using striking symbolic acts as a means of appealing to hardened sinners who had turned a deaf ear to their words" (Voight 338). Voight cites biblical examples such as Jeremiah's wearing the yoke as representative of the prophet's understanding of sins the Israelites were committing and Ezekiel shaving his head and face to foreshadow the destruction or dispersal of the wicked in Jerusalem. Voight goes on to explain that, "like the symbolic acts of the Hebrew prophets, Hooper's wearing of the black veil leant strange power to his warnings to callous sinners, even though he, like the ancient prophets, had to pay for this power the costly price of misunderstanding, loneliness, and agony of soul" (Voight 338). Voight highlights the validity of drawing comparisons with the Hebrew Bible in Hawthorne's work, citing references to Israelite prophets in other works such as *The Scarlet Letter*. Voight's proposal for a parallel with the symbolic actions of biblical prophets supports Hooper's isolation, and it lays a solid foundation for developing the connections between Hooper and prophetic actions.

A 1962 article by Robert Cochran, "Hawthorne's Choice: The Veil or the Jaundiced Eye," emphasizes New Testament themes and offers a salient point about the ambiguous nature of the genre of parable: "Hawthorne called 'The Minister's Black Veil' a 'parable,' and one purpose of a parable is to clarify. The parable of the veil clarifies not simply by mirroring the ambiguity of life in a parallel ambiguity of meaning...but also by identifying the source of life's ambiguity" (Cochran, 344). Cochran's emphasis on the centrality of ambiguity in parables is productive, and he develops the idea of mystery in a way that aligns with the isolating experience of the prophets: "Father Hooper becomes a man apart, in that for him the secret of sin lies in its mysterious depths and not in a sense of particular shame or guilt" (344). Although Cochran's analysis moves toward a somewhat limited, specifically Christian, reading of Hawthorne's fiction, he sees mystery as central to Hooper's action.

Some subsequent critics have developed the relationships between "The Minister's Black Veil" and biblical themes by drawing specific interpretations of the veil. Judy McCarthy argues for an interesting fusion of Moses and Christ in the person of Hooper, comparing the minister's veil with that worn by Moses, as described earlier in this chapter (McCarthy, "'The Minister's Black Veil': Concealing Moses and the Holy of Holies," 131). McCarthy reads Hooper's sad smile, often described as seeming to "glimmer," as one indication of the parallel (133). But in asserting that "Moses' veil symbolically points to the unseen salvation of Christ," (134)[2] McCarthy concludes that, "Hooper chooses the outward veil, signifying Christ, as opposed to the inward veil of separation from Christ. In choosing to veil his face, he removes the veil from his heart" (137). While McCarthy's readings of the symbolism of the veil are provocative, her somewhat reductive interpretations contradict the terror inherent in the mystery, the inexplicability of the veil. Never-

---

[2] McCarthy's reading is an argument against William Stein's analysis that the message of the veil is a rejection of the gospel of the New Testament, particularly 2 Corinthians 3, which takes up the reinterpretation of Moses' veil.

theless, she rightly asserts that, "the language of the text resists easy compartmentalization" (132).

Frederick Newberry's reading moves in the opposite direction of McCarthy's, claiming that, "whatever correspond-
ence Hooper has to Moses must ultimately be seen as ironic,
his veil declaring his separation from God rather than imply-
ing a personal if hidden access to the light of the Lord's presence" (Newberry, 189). Newberry views Hooper as fixated on
doubt and sin rather than salvation: if a message is discerna-
ble, it is of a reversal of the Christian path to redemption
(189). Others have explored biblical tropes and imagery in
"The Minister's Black Veil," and while most promote compelling interpretations, they tend to draw somewhat com-
partmentalized or reductive conclusions.

The story's genre, the parable, nonetheless invites the
audience to speculate regarding the meaning or moral of the
story. The basic definition of a parable is that which "signifies a comparison; literally it is something cast (ballo βαλλω)
alongside (para παρα)" (Hedrick, *NIDB* 377). In the biblical
context, the parable generally has both a surface meaning and
a deeper religious significance: "early Christian literature appears to designate as 'parable' any saying of Jesus whose
meaning is not immediately clear in terms of Christian faith
and theology...[W]hat appears to be banal language is
judged to be figurative or comparative discourse and is given
a deeper significance" (Hedrick 369). Parables intentionally
spark multiple possible interpretations, and to explain a parable conclusively would defeat one of its central purposes: to
engage the audience with the power of religious mystery.

In his foundational work on parables, *Parables of the
Kingdom*, C. H. Dodd defines the New Testament parable as

"a metaphor or simile drawn from nature or common life, arresting the hearer by its vividness or strangeness, and leaving the mind in sufficient doubt about its precise application to tease it into active thought" (5).[3] Few distinctions exist between the Hebrew Bible parable, מָשָׁל (*mashal*), and the New Testament parable (παραβολή), the New Testament parable deriving many of its characteristics from Hebrew and other ancient near eastern traditions. In the Hebrew Bible, *mashal* is a broader genre, denoting a variety of "literary units whose meaning is not immediately clear or easily understood" (Hedrick 368).[4] The New Testament parable, which is what Hawthorne and his readers would connect with the word *parable*, is intended more specifically to challenge the hearer.[5] The parable is far more common in the New Testament than it is in the Hebrew Bible.

In addition to being ambiguous, parables can intentionally work to conceal. Consider Jesus' strange words in Mark 4:10–12:

---

[3] On the hermeneutics of parables see Norman Perrin, *Parable and Gospel* 35–50.

[4] "In general, mashal is used to designate narratives (Ezek 17:2–10), brief figures (Ezek 24:3–5), traditional proverbs (1 Sam 24:13; Ezek 18:2), laments cast as brief narratives (Ezek 19-1-9), and sayings (Mic 2:4; Hab 2:5–6). Mashal is also used as a parallel to the RIDDLE…, which is also a type of obscure or enigmatic speech" (Hedrick 368).

Parables belong to the wisdom genre. See James L. Crenshaw, *Old Testament Wisdom: An Introduction*, and Roland E. Murphy, *Wisdom Literature: Job, Proverbs, Ruth, Canticles, Ecclesiastes, and Ester* 3-12.

> And when he was alone, they that were about him
> with the twelve asked of him the parable. And he said
> unto them, Unto you it is given to know the mystery
> of the kingdom of God: but unto them that are with-
> out, all these things are done in parables: That seeing
> they may see, and not perceive; and hearing they may
> hear, and not understand; lest at any time they should
> be converted, and their sins should be forgiven them.

This is a famously challenging passage. It suggests that the purpose of a parable is to conceal, or at least to conceal in part. Those who "are without" will not understand the parables or will receive a surface understanding at best; however, they will not glean the valuable part of the parable's message. Moreover, the enigmatic nature of the parable will serve to prevent sinners from converting and being forgiven. Does Jesus genuinely wish outsiders to be prevented from receiving forgiveness here, or do his words have an ironic cast? Jesus' message of forgiveness for outcasts and sinners throughout the gospels supports an ironic interpretation of his words. But in prompting us to think the message through, the parable has done its job of engaging the audience by its challenging or mysterious message. This implies the active use of the mind or imagination for discernment: "knowing" is not to be had without effort (Hudspeth, 30 September 2009).

Though we frequently identify parables with Jesus, this discourse on parables stands solidly in the prophetic tradition, as Mark 4:10–12 is an allusion to Isaiah 6:9–10:

> And he said, Go, and tell this people, Hear ye in-
> deed, but understand not; and see ye indeed, but
> perceive not. Make the heart of this people fat, and
> make their ears heavy, and shut their eyes; lest they

see with their eyes, and hear with their ears, and understand with their heart, and convert, and be healed.

In citing this passage from Isaiah, Jesus is appealing to the prophetic literature—and in turn offering a twice-told tale. The line that Jesus omits: "Make the heart of this people fat, and make their ears heavy, and shut their eyes," further ensures that the people misunderstand the message. God's words, spoken through the prophet Isaiah, tell of the punishment they will endure because of their faithlessness. This passage echoes other challenging narratives about God's disabling powers, such as Exodus 9:12, in which, after Pharaoh hardened his own heart two times, the third time it is God who hardens Pharaoh's heart. Perhaps this passage, and in turn the Markan pericope, conveys the trajectory of the human capacity to listen to a challenging message: when eyes and ears close, the ability to reverse the process, to adapt a compassionate stance, decreases. So starts a downward spiral of comprehending less and less, until what was once willfully misunderstanding a certain message has become second nature, and a kind of surrender.

Another reason why a speaker of parables might want to conceal their meaning is so that people hostile to the message would not gain an upper hand. This is the case for Jesus throughout the New Testament in which communities such as the Sadducees viewed him as "a direct threat to their civil and religious authority" (Stein, 33). In conveying a mysterious message, "Jesus made it difficult for his opponents to bring meaningful charges and accusations against him" (Stein, 34). Applying this to "The Minister's Black Veil" would suggest that Hooper is keeping himself safe from potentially destructive accusations by his Puritan community, such as the confession of specific sins might prompt, and the Puritan tradition of persecution renders this a possibility. But the veil also brings a quality of seriousness to the minister's plight. Though it is a simple square of fabric, no one dares remove it from his face. Whether or not the veil pushes people away or draws them toward the minister, the mystery of the veil, like the mystery of a parable, elicits a degree of awe in the Puritan community.

Parables also serve to move listeners by disarming them: "At times Jesus sought to penetrate the hostility and hardness of heart of his listeners by means of a parable. The famous parable of Nathan in 2 Sam 12:1–4 is a perfect Old Testament example of this" (Stein, 35). After King David commits adultery with Bathsheba, Uriah's wife, he has Uriah killed. Following these actions, the prophet Nathan presents a parable to the king.[6] Nathan tells of a poor man who has nothing but a small lamb that he loves and feeds with his hand. A neighboring rich man, who owns many sheep, takes and kills the poor man's only lamb in order to serve a wandering visitor. Without realizing that the cruel actions of the rich man of the parable represent his own adulterous and murderous behavior, David declares that such a man should be killed and the lamb should be restored to the poor man fourfold. Nathan then tells David that the parable is about

---

[6] Nathan's parable, along with 2 Samuel 14:5–7 and Ecclesiastes 9:14–15, is one of the three Hebrew Bible narratives that come closest to the parables of Jesus: "these narratives do not use cryptic language but reflect a mimetic fictional realism" (Hedrick, 369).

him: "Thou art the man" (2 Sam 12:7). Because David had grown so passionately involved in the parable, he is unable to retract his declarations, must admit his own wrong, and ask God's forgiveness. It is through confessing his sinfulness that David regains God's support.[7] Thus, as much as a parable can confuse and estrange, it can also engross and transform.

Reactions including confusion and transformation also figure among the spectrum of responses to Hooper's veil. Some members of the community are offended or alarmed by the veil and avoid the minister at all costs. Others are arrested by the strange veil and become devotes of the Puritan minister. Many have the sense that the veiled minister can perceive their secret sins. Those who follow Hooper in open admission of their sinful nature, and in acceptance of the mystery of the veil, seem to be the most religiously fulfilled. In contrast, those who resist or are skeptical of the mystery remain frustrated.

Negative community responses to Hooper's veil suggest the tragic nature of this parable. Dan Otto Via applies the categories of comedy and tragedy to Jesus' parables, reminding the reader that "in comedy we have an upward movement toward wellbeing and the inclusion of the protagonist in a new or renewed society, while in tragedy we have a plot fall-

---

[7] See Anthony F. Campbell, *2 Samuel*, 116–118. "The brilliance of Nathan's parable is that its thinking is so lateral it almost misses the mark—and so takes David by surprise" (116). This parable is suited to a farming community in which sheep stealing "may be almost as close to the ultimate crime against humanity as one is likely to get" (116). The closer the parable to the context of the audience, the more likely they are to be moved by it.

ing toward catastrophe and the isolation of the protagonist from society" (Via, *The Parables: Their Literary and Existential Dimension*, 96). Many of Jesus' parables fall into one of these categories, the Prodigal Son being an example of a comic parable, and the Ten Maidens, five of whom are ultimately excluded from the wedding feast, being an example of a tragic parable. In tragic parables "we see a plot falling toward disappointment and isolation from a joyous society" (Via, 97). "The Minister's Black Veil" is thus tragedy, as the protagonist grows isolated from his community. As Via explains, "in the tragic vision there is a necessary and inescapable fatal defect in the relationship between an undertaken purpose and the protagonist's world. What he attempts inevitably leads to suffering" (Via, 111). Nevertheless, the protagonist feels obligated to take this path, as he values morality over happiness: "That the tragic hero dies or suffers matters little since he saves his authentic self by refusing to sink into second-hand morality" (Via, 111).

The symbolic actions of the biblical prophets regularly take place in the context of tragedy as well. God commands Ezekiel to lie on his right side for three hundred and ninety days not for relaxation, but to bear the sins of Israel: "Lie thou also upon thy left side, and lay the iniquity of the house of Israel upon it: according to the number of the days that thou shalt lie upon it thou shalt bear their iniquity" (Ezekiel 4:4). God commands Ezekiel to prepare his food over a dung fire as a sign that the temple has become utterly corrupt (Ezekiel 4:12–15). The symbolic actions of Ezekiel and other prophets reflect the ways in which humanity has sinned against God.[8] They also have literary significance. The text does not always describe their being carried out, and the actions described are not always feasible (Hals, *Ezekiel*, 30). In Ezekiel, symbolic actions regularly function as powerful literary devices. Indeed, "some symbolic actions are elaborated so extensively in the sections in which interpretation appears that the boundary between the symbolic action and literary elaboration in another genre is crossed over" (Hals, 30). The power of the action, then, is largely literary. As Hals further explains, "instead of seeing symbolic action as a pedagogical addendum to the spoken word, it has become clear that the action is itself a powerful word. Symbolic actions constitute a creatively forceful prefiguring of future events, so that the future event begins to happen in and is guaranteed by the symbolic action" (Hals, 33). Hals notes that part of the literary power of Ezekiel's symbolic actions derives from the detail that goes into them. As such, "their stress is on power, not on clarification by illustration" (Hals, 34). The power inherent in the action is primary; an explanation of the exact reasoning behind the minutia of the action is not.

Ezekiel offers some explanation of his symbolic actions, but the explanation is not exhaustive, nor is it the point of the action. Hooper offers even less explanation of his action, though he does gesture toward it. He speaks of the community as reflected in the somber veil, telling Elizabeth that, "There is an hour to come...when all of us shall cast aside

---

[8] Ezekiel's symbolic actions resonate with David Stacey's model for symbolic actions in *Prophetic Drama in the Old Testament* (Epworth Press), 1990, which will be discussed in more detail later in this chapter.

our veils" (46). At his death bed he declares, "I look around me, and, lo! on every visage a Black Veil!" (52). Hooper describes the community as wearing metaphorical veils, and in turn, as participating in the same state of existence for which he wears the veil. These lines suggest that Hooper has not committed a sin for which he alone is guilty, but that he acts as the representative of a community in tragic circumstances.

In light of this, the connection between Hooper's action and the symbolic actions of the biblical prophets is a fruitful source of comparison. In the biblical context, the prophet generally carries out a symbolic action to instill a divine message in himself, or to convey a message to the community. The symbolic action is "intentionally employed in the proclamation of the prophetic message so as to communicate, through the non-verbal channel, a message to an audience" (Friebel, "A Hermeneutical Paradigm for Interpreting Prophetic Sign-Actions," 25, n. 1). The symbolic action can serve several purposes. It can depict something that will come to pass or a warning about something that may take place if the people do not modify their current behaviors or perspectives. Kelvin Fribel explains that, of the prophetic symbolic actions, we most often encounter

> the paradigm of "inherent efficaciousness" or "causal link." The effectiveness of the sign-act is perceived as causally setting the depicted event in motion through the very performance of the act...[which]... "releases an event in miniature, it says that a particular consequence is not simply possible, not simply predictable, it is unavoidable because it is already in being...it is the release of an inevitable cir-

cumstance which nothing can avert." (Bowker 130 as qtd. in Friebel 29)[9]

For example, in Jeremiah 27-28, when Babylon is gaining power, God commands Jeremiah to wear a yoke and to inform surrounding nations that they too must serve under the yoke of the Babylonian king. At some future time, the tables will turn and Nebuchadnezzar will be subjected by other nations.[10] Yet for now, the narrative states that God has handed power to Babylon and the wearing of the yokes "releases an event in miniature," as it were. Thus, a future-oriented message is frequently associated with the symbolic action, and it can precede either a possible or an imminent event, both of which are usually negative. In either of these cases, the symbolic action represents, to varying degrees, the future event.[11]

Yet a symbolic action can also be, and often is, a form of commentary on a current situation or behavior that originated in the past and is ongoing or has already taken place. For example, as a representation of the sinfulness of the Israelites, the prophet Hosea writes that he marries an unfaithful prostitute, Gomer, in order to embody the way in which Israel has sinned and continues to sin against YHWH by wor-

---

[9] See also David Stacey, *Prophetic Drama in the Old Testament.*

[10] On Jeremiah's Yoke see Jack R. Lundbom, *Jeremiah 21-36: A New Translation with Introduction and Commentary,* 302–342 and Leslie C. Allen, *Jeremiah: A Commentary,* 302–319.

[11] For further scholarly analysis of Jeremiah see Louis Stulman, *Jeremiah.*

shipping other gods.[12] In various contexts, the symbolic action can be understood as meaning, "just as the prophet has done, so it has been done by the audience, or will be done to them, or should be done by them" (Friebel, 26). Finally, the symbolic action, an expression of God's concern or will regarding God's people, is carried out to warn, instruct, condemn, or simply assert the relationship between God and humanity; it has a kerygmatic function.

Turning to "The Minister's Black Veil," it could be said that Hooper's wearing of the black veil has a kerygmatic, or preaching, function. And yet, if that is the case, why has Hawthorne left the specific meaning of the veil ambiguous? Unlike many of the prophetic books, Hawthorne's tale offers no dialogue between God and the one carrying out the sym-

---

[12] The example of Hosea reminds the reader to be wary of taking the symbolic action at face value. Though scholars have long accepted Hosea's word for the unfaithfulness and prostitute status of Gomer, feminist scholars such as Frances Landy remind us that the narrative never offers Gomer's perspective (See Landy, *Hosea* 23–24). Sweeney notes that considering the experience of the accused is particularly relevant "as YHWH accuses Israel of infidelity throughout the book, and yet it is YHWH who will bring the Assyrians to punish Israel. Israel was destroyed by the Assyrians, and the book of Hosea explains this reality theologically by arguing that Israel sinned against YHWH. Hosea raises a question of theodicy to the modern reader in a personally pointed way, viz., did Israel sin by failing to be true to YHWH, or did YHWH sin by failing to be true to Israel?" (Sweeney, *The Twelve Prophets*, vol. 1, 6). Regarding the issue of presuppositions in Hosea scholarship, see Gale A. Yee, *Composition and Tradition in the Book of Hosea* 27–50.

bolic action. There is a silent voice in the narrative, no matter where we locate it. We cannot decisively conclude that the minister's action is the carrying out of God's will, or even if Hooper believes that he is carrying out God's will. Yet, based on Hooper's sympathetic, steady character, his respected position in the community before the story begins, his revulsion to his own veiled image when he glances in the mirror, and his distress at being ostracized by the community, we can assume, at the least, that he does not wear the veil for pleasure.[13] Indeed, based on the character clues given, such a tempered, pious clergyman would not go to such drastic measures unless his act had some kind of kerygmatic function, either for himself or for the community. Like the prophets, he appears moved by a powerful, outside force. But what is the message his symbolic action is meant to convey and why does he neither inform the community of the message of the veil, nor remove it? The impossibility of directly answering these questions reflects Hawthorne's concern with mystery. The ultimate inscrutability of the human heart, "that saddest of all prisons" (50), haunts this text.

---

[13] Not every critic agrees with this view. For example, Michael Davitt Bell posits the interesting, if unlikely, reading that Hooper wears the veil, among other things, to avoid marrying Elizabeth: "Hooper seems to do more than simply accept separation from Elizabeth and mankind; he seems positively to desire such separation. 'This dismal shade,' he shouts almost gleefully to Elizabeth, 'must separate me from the world: even you, Elizabeth, can never come behind it!'" (*Hawthorne and the Historical Romance of New England*, 66).

The first information Hawthorne offers about the symbolic action is what it is not. In the footnote to the sub-title, "A Parable," the narrator explains that this parable grew out of an actual account in which a clergyman, eighty years prior to the writing of the tale, performed the same symbolic action of donning a black veil. "In his case, however, the symbol had a different import," which was to hide his face for the remainder of his life after having killed his friend accidentally (37). Hawthorne will not tell us the meaning of the veil, but he gives us a clue: what we can know *specifically* is that Hooper does *not* wear the veil for having killed a friend on accident. Although it may seem easy enough to draw more implications for the meaning of the veil from what is given in the footnote, only one specific explanation has been eliminated, and related meanings *may* be implied.

Returning to biblical paradigms, another characteristic of the prophetic symbolic action is that it usually provides an awkward or unpleasant experience for the audience or community. It would also seem to be so for the prophet himself, because the symbolic actions are invariably unpleasant. However, the biblical writers rarely describe the unpleasantness of undergoing a symbolic action.[14] The biblical prophet generally carries out the divinely ordained nonverbal action with little questioning of his assignment, though there is of course a biblical tradition of reluctant prophets, such as Jonah, and

---

[14] One example of a prophet remarking on the unpleasantness of a symbolic sign action command is when Ezekiel protests God's command that he cook barley cakes over a fire of human dung. God relents, allowing Ezekiel to use cow dung instead (Ezekiel 4:12–15).

Ezekiel rejects the command that he cook over dung (Ezek. 4:12–15). But if the action is one that is experienced by the audience, the experience of encountering the sign-action is invariably jolting for the community. One quality of the future-oriented sign action, for example, is its temporal disordering: "sign acts brought the future into the present" (Friebel 30), which would be a jarring experience. In this light, the act disrupts temporally as well as socially; it brings forth warning, comment, or condemnation to a community not yet, or ever, ready to yield to the message.

The expression, *the prophetic perfect* (tense) describes the unique relationship with time that many prophetic writings employ. The prophetic perfect can be used to project what might happen in the future. It can also represent a kind of eternal present. As is particularly the case with Ezekiel, for example, elements of mythology and creation loom large in this prophet's purview. As the less temporally bound mythological expressions associated with creation indicate a connection with God, the mythological world operates as an insight into the heavenly world. Differing notions of time and place affect the text, and "real" time-bound issues, such as whether a particular prophetic oracle took place in historical "reality" as described, lose substantial relevancy. In operating out of this kind of prophetic perfect, God, through the prophet, writes words that not only speak to the prophet's experience of reality, but also broader truths about the nature of mystery and the character of God (Sweeney, 8 May 2007).

Nevertheless, later readers of sign act literature can more easily appreciate the wisdom of strange actions than would a prophet's contemporaries at whom the action is directed. Hooper's community, unused to encountering alternative representations of reality, cringes at the strange action. Town gatherings and rituals that were once pleasurable, such as weddings, are all but ruined in the eyes of the townspeople by the minister's ominous black veil. The men, who are agitated to the degree that they organize a committee to question Hooper, are unable even to state their concerns when faced with the terrifying veil. Yet the question persists: if Hooper's action is intended to move the community in some way, what is he trying to persuade them to do or think? This question remains unanswered, and so it is unlikely that the symbolic action falls entirely under the category of a future-oriented warning.

Still, our evasive narrator has the minister gesture toward a kind of prophetic perfect at the end of his life. Hooper's final words, spoken on his deathbed, point to the veil's possible implications:

> "Why do you tremble at me alone?" cried he, turning his veiled face round the circle of pale spectators. "Tremble also at each other! Have men avoided me, and women shown no pity, and children screamed and fled, only for my black veil? What, but the mystery which it obscurely typifies, has made this piece of crape so awful? When the friend shows his inmost heart to his friend; the lover to his best-beloved; when man does not vainly shrink from the eye of his Creator, loathsomely treasuring up the secret of his sin; then deem me a monster, for the symbol beneath which I have lived, and die! I look around me, and, lo! on every visage a Black Veil!" (52)

Past, present, and future are bound in this final message about how people have and continue to respond to the veil. Again, the veil's lack of understandable meaning is what engenders its power and its horrifying impact. The mythical truths behind the prophetic perfect message are that friends and lovers should be open with each other, and humanity should not shrink from God, "loathsomely treasuring up the secret of his sin."

It is interesting to note that all the accusations Hooper issues in this final speech could equally be applied to himself as well as his community. For, insofar as he offers only evasive explanations of the veil to Elizabeth, and little to none to the rest of the community, he does not share his inmost heart with his friends or his beloved (though we are not privy to what his relationship with his Creator may be). Perhaps the minister himself does not know exactly why he is compelled to wear the veil. Perhaps explaining any more about the veil is somehow impossible, and with the story's central focus on obscurity, this may well be the case. Thus, the lack of true connection that seems to be an inherent aspect of the mortal world, which will always exist, is a part of the mystery of the veil.

One more applicable paradigm scholars have used to explore the disruptive aspects of a prophetic act is the "street theater" paradigm (Lang, "Street Theater: Raising the Dead, and the Zoroastrian Connection in Ezekiel's Prophecy," 297). This paradigm offers a way to understand the abrasive, or even offensive experience of encountering the prophet carrying out the symbolic action. Akin to the image of an activist on the proverbial soapbox, the "street theater" paradigm presents the nonverbal action as offering "ways and means of obtaining a hearing for a message which is sometimes less than desirable and frequently far from flattering" (Lang, "Monotheism and the Prophetic Minority," 88–89). It highlights the symbolic action as a method for agitating a complacent or misguided community. This paradigm emphasizes the centrality of persuasion and interaction with the community; it is not so much about communicating information as it is moving the crowd to a new perspective or course of action.[15] The "street theater" paradigm can be helpful in interpreting Hooper's symbolic action insofar as his wearing the veil makes many of the members of his community considerably uncomfortable.

Central to the impact of Hawthorne's narrative is the impenetrable mystery of the veil. Yet we can and should strive to approach that mystery. In this regard the paradigms for examining symbolic actions, and in particular the *form critical* paradigms, are appropriate. The form critical approach to biblical studies is concerned primarily with the way in which a particular narrative has been presented in its final form, and the way that form conveys meaning, power, aesthetics, etc. An example of a common analytical approach that is not concerned with the final form of a text is redaction criticism. Redaction critics study the various layers that make up a biblical text and how and when they were edited together to create the final form of the text.[16] Form criticism,

---

[15] E.g., the persuasive words of the prophet Micaiah in 1 Kings 22.

[16] For a foundational treatment of redaction criticism see Norman Perrin, *What is Redaction Criticism* (13–24: form criticism as precursor to redaction criticism). Form criticism "is concerned

however, operates more like literary criticism, tracing and analyzing the nuances and literary features of the text in its final form.[17] In fact, form criticism grew out of literary criticism, "for which the determination of the structure or composition of larger literary works (the sources) was a major ingredient of methodology" (Knierim, "Criticism of Literary Features, Form, Tradition, and Redaction," 136). Within the sphere of form critical approaches to the biblical text, David Stacey's work, *Prophetic Drama in the Old Testament*, establishes a mode for approaching symbolic actions. For example, he addresses the issue of discrepancies between the prophet's intention and the degree to which the audience understands that action:

> How an action is understood demands the question: understood by whom? The prophet may have one intention, but the onlookers may infer that intention incorrectly. And a distinction must be made between the inferences of sophisticated observers,

---

with studying the theological motivation of an author as this is revealed in the collection, arrangement, editing, and modification of traditional material, and in the composition of new material or the creation of new forms within the traditions of early Christianity" (Perrin, 1).

[17] For foundational treatments of form criticism see Rolf Knierim, "Criticism of Literary Features, Form, Tradition, and Redaction" in *The Hebrew Bible and Its Modern Interpreters*, esp. 136–146; and Marvin A. Sweeney, "Isaiah 1-4 and the Post-Exilic Understanding of the Isaianic Tradition," esp. 54–89 for an explanation of the history and limitations of redaction criticism, and the elements and advantages of form criticism.

familiar with the prophet's message and its theological context, and those of the common people whom we must suppose to have been unsophisticated, not to say downright superstitious, in their religious understanding. (Stacey, 5–6)

While Stacey is of course speaking to the situation of the biblical prophet, this description of the concern with communal response to the symbolic action can be applied to "The Minister's Black Veil" as well. Hawthorne is careful to give us different responses to Hooper's symbolic action: some people avoid him; others taunt him; still others become his devotees. Elizabeth falls under the category of "sophisticated observers," as she appears able, not to understand the veil, but to continue to face it throughout life and in nursing him at his deathbed. Similarly, Hooper's devotees call for his presence at their deathbeds, though "as he stooped to whisper consolation, they shuddered at the veiled face so near their own. Such were the terrors of the black veil, even when Death had bared his visage!" (49). While it is not stated that Elizabeth or the devotees understand the veil, it is their asserting a closeness to the minister in his awful veil that distinguishes them from others in the community.

The acceptance of mystery does not bring joy or satisfaction, but those who grant Hooper religious authority by devoting themselves to him are depicted more positively than those who shun Hooper and his veil. The mystery of the veil puts a psychological burden on the parishioners that many of them cannot stand. One of the signs of their not being able to live in its proximity is their continual questioning of what it means. (We may also say this for literary scholars who strain to uncover the veil's meaning.) The veil is not about being understood, but about being able to live in proximity with its awful obscurity, or to seek to live truly in the face of mystery. To avoid living superficially, the best the parishioners can do is accept the unknowability of the veil, of the world, of the heart.

Our analytical approach to Hawthorne's short story is thus guided by the parameters of a form critical approach to prophetic literature, in which a central place is reserved for the role of mystery. To that end, Stacey cautions against assuming singular interpretations: "To suppose, therefore, that a simple and universal 'explanation' of prophetic drama is there to be discovered is a great error. This does not make the present enquiry useless, but it complicates the undertaking and imposes limits on our expectations" (Stacey 6). The panoply of specific "explanations" for the black veil in scholarly criticism is evidence enough that this tendency should be checked. While Hawthorne invites us to speculate on the power the veil has over the various characters in the story, and indeed on our own reactions to it, he intentionally frustrates our attempts to draw conclusive readings of it.

Taking this notion further, Stacey explores the issue of meaning itself when looking at prophetic texts. He reminds us that "there is the philosophical problem of the relation of action to meaning. What is the precise force of the word 'meaning' when it is predicated of a piece of dramatic action?" (Stacey, 6–7). This is a valuable question that readers of Hawthorne's story should bear in mind. For Hawthorne calls into question our relationship to the notion of "meaning." It is the townspeople's shortsighted eagerness for a specific meaning to ascribe to the veil that could be seen as their downfall. Just as Stacey warns biblical scholars "to beware of overconfidence when trying to define explicit meanings for actions," the nature of Hawthorne's work is such that we should yield ourselves to the text, allow ourselves to dwell in the uncomfortable realm of its obscurity (Stacey, 7). Stacey advocates the avoidance of dogmatic explanations, and limiting our readings to those that are "tentative and never precise" (Stacey, 7). Yet in striving to avoid dogmatic explanations, we may assert truths about topics that can be difficult to describe, such as ambiguity. In other words, we need not be "tentative and never precise" about the role of mystery. Rather, as Stacey wisely asserts, "disciplined imagination is necessary and valuable" (Stacey, 8).[18]

Because mystery can be associated with, if not the divine, alternative planes of reality, such guidelines for a responsible form critical approach to biblical analysis are appropriate. For, while the narrative blocks our attempts to form comfortable conclusions and theories, the mystery of the veil nonetheless exists as the central, shaping concern of the text. In biblical literature we find struggles to understand God, evil, why things happen as they do, etc. Hawthorne

---

[18] Other elements of Stacey's advice for the interpretation of biblical prophetic actions that lend themselves well to Hawthorne's text include the call for "a conscious attempt to let the text speak for itself and not to order the investigation in the way most positive for confessional interpretation" (9). Likewise problematic is "the confidence that everything in Scripture can be explained, that obscurities have only to be noted and analyzed for their mysteries to be resolved" (9). Both Hawthorne and Scriptural studies challenge our ability to account for mystery, to make space for unsettling obscurity at the center of a text.

wrestled with these issues too. Perhaps his primary concern is not so much the desire for an answer to the mystery as it is a genuine struggle with mystery.

This struggle is seen in Reverend Hooper's own response to his wearing of the black veil. He is saddened by the way it isolates him from his community that once appreciated his role in various liturgical and communal events. That the veil isolates him from Elizabeth can be seen as another layer of his own response to the veil. Hooper's sad smile reflects his reaction to those of his community. His final action on his deathbed of physically preventing his veil from being removed is another facet of Hooper's response to his wearing of the veil and his commitment to bearing this "burden." Obscurity shapes all these events. If there is one aspect of the veil that the reader, Hooper, Elizabeth, and indeed most of the community agree upon about the veil, is the encounter it forces with unknowability. Obscurity is there from beginning to end, and it is that which engenders the terror of the veil.

When Hooper mounts the pulpit on the first day he wears the veil, the veil's shadowy quality is described: "That mysterious emblem was never once withdrawn. It shook with his measured breath as he gave out the psalm; it threw its obscurity between him and the holy page...Did he seek to hide it from the dread Being whom he was addressing?" (39). From almost the first moments the community encounters their veiled minister, and he emerges faceless before them, the veil is "mysterious." It possesses an active power to cloak the relationship between the minister and the people, the minister and the Scripture, and the minister and his prayers: "it *threw* its obscurity between him and the holy page" (my emphasis). Almost as though the veil were a sentient entity, it creates a disquieting presence in the midst of the community as it blurs and disfigures once comfortable relationships. Discussing the unsettling effect of the veil with his wife, the town physician confesses that, "the strangest part of the affair is the effect of this vagary, even on a sober-minded man like myself. The black veil, though it covers only our pastor's face, throws its influence over his whole person, and makes him ghost-like from head to foot" (41). This effect of vagary affects the townspeople in different ways. For the sensible physician who considers himself to be "sober-minded," the very vagary, rather than any superstitious implications, is that which is unsettling. Indeed, though some of the townspeople are described as "superstitious," and there exists variety in their responses, they are generally characterized as good, decent people who, after the first day of good Reverend Hooper's wearing of the veil, "talked of little else than Parson Hooper's black veil. That, and the mystery concealed behind it" (44).

Still, the mysterious quality of the veil, though universally acknowledged by the community, is more projected or speculated than it is directly asserted. When the townspeople hold a meeting to address the issue of the veil, they are, interestingly, unable to speak, and "that piece of crape, to their imagination, seemed to hang down before his heart, the symbol of a fearful secret between him and them" (45). Hawthorne is interested in the effect of the veil on the townspeople: the mystery of the veil destabilizes them to such a degree that they are unable to address the subject of the veil, or even to speak. But there is one person, Hooper's betrothed, who, at least at first, "could discern nothing of the dreadful gloom that had so overawed the multitude: it was but a double fold of crape, hanging down from his forehead to his mouth, and slightly stirring with his breath" (45). Calm and strong, Elizabeth is the only one who directly addresses him about the veil and is not initially moved by any awful sense of mystery or obscurity. But during the interview, a transformation seems to take place in her. After Hooper refuses either to remove the veil or directly answer to its specific meaning, Elizabeth sits in silence and gives way to tears.

> But, in an instant, as it were, a new feeling took the place of sorrow: her eyes were fixed insensibly on the black veil, when, like a sudden twilight in the air, its terrors fell around her. She arose, and stood trembling before him.
>
> 'And do you feel it then at last?' said he mournfully.
>
> She made no reply, but covered her eyes with her hand, and turned to leave the room. (47)

Has Elizabeth indeed felt the meaning of the veil, or has she rather begun to imagine the awful of quality of obscurity that the other townspeople feel? Has she arrived at a realization that there is no sense in responding? At any rate, Hooper's comment raises questions about the nature of the veil's power. It is when Elizabeth starts, visibly terror stricken, that Hooper wonders if she can "feel it." From this we can know two things about the veil: that, rightly perceived, it elicits a kind of terror or awe from the individual, and its power is something that can be *felt*. It may be that while the perceived horror of Hooper's parishioners may arise out of their own imaginings about the veil, it is that horror which the veil is intended to produce. It becomes tempting to speculate at this point. For example, might the veil have been a test for which, once Elizabeth consented to marry him despite the veil, he would have removed the veil? (After all, this is a parable.) Might the veil represent Hooper's sin in having had an affair with the maiden at whose funeral Hooper officiates? Central to the narrative is that it is impossible to say. For Hawthorne is invested in the notion of impossibility; he has purposefully created a narrative in which the townsperson, the reader, the literary critic, must respond either with projected assumptions about the veil's meaning, or dwell uncomfortably, yet genuinely, in the prophetic mystery.

This "miserable obscurity" of the veil, as Hooper describes it himself, seems to be the source and power of the veil. Hawthorne allows us to speculate about the fact that the veil may be nothing more than the black crape that Elizabeth at first perceives, until her onset of terror leads Hooper to ask if she can "feel it" too. This has nothing to do with intellect. The "mystery" of the veil is not something that can be intellectually understood, for it terrorizes even Hooper himself; it is something that can be felt. Iain Duguid speaks to the feeling a sign action is meant to elicit; they are "complex acted-out parables. These signs are not merely visual aids; they are designed to reach people's wills and hearts, enabling people not just to see the truth but to feel it" (Duguid, "Did a Prophet Really Lay on His Side for More than a Year? (Ezekiel 4)"). As such, the mystery with which the veil horrifies everyone would seem to be exactly what they are meant to experience. In that sense, it is not a mystery that is meant to be discovered or understood; it is in existing as an enigma that the veil is effective.[19]

And it is that power that magnifies the effectiveness of Hooper's preaching. If reverend Hooper's symbolic action is intended to stir his parishioners to piety, he succeeds in abundance. The very first sermon that Hooper preaches after donning the veil is about "secret sin, and those sad mysteries which we hide form our nearest and dearest" (40). On its own, this is an evocative topic, but paired with the veil Hooper commands tremendous power over the congregation:

> A subtle power was breathed into his words. Each member of the congregation, the most innocent girl, and the man of hardened breast, felt as if the preacher had crept upon them, behind his awful veil, and discovered their hoarded iniquity of deed or thought. Many spread their clasped hands on their bosoms. There was nothing terrible in what Mr. Hooper said; at least, no violence; and yet, with every tremor of his melancholy voice, the hearers quaked. An unsought pathos came hand in hand with awe. (40)

---

[19] A related biblical example might be the imagery of theophany, of God in the cloud as in Exodus 19 and 20. The Hebrew term עֲרָפֶּל (araphael), meaning *deep darkness*, describes God's location in theophanic texts, as in the center of a cloud or storm: "And the people stood afar off, and Moses drew near unto *the thick darkness* (הָעֲרָפֶּל) where God was" (Exodus 20:21).

Like a prophet carrying out a successful symbolic action, Hooper stirs his community, and himself, out of their comfortable spheres and into a new place of disquieting awareness. The encounter with the veil moves the people to look inward and to feel as though their deepest secret sins are exposed. They are awe-struck and overwhelmed with a pathos they did not seek. Like a biblical prophet, Hooper and his veil lead the people to a sense that he possesses the capabilities of divination, that he has access to their innermost thoughts.

Later that day, the presence of Hooper in his veil at the funeral stirs the people with a heightened gloom. Although the narrator explains that in the context of the funeral, the veil "was now an appropriate emblem," (42) it nevertheless casts a new heaviness and disquieting mystery on the proceedings: "The people trembled, though they but darkly understood him, when he prayed that they, and himself, and all of mortal race, might be ready, and he trusted this young maiden had been, for the dreadful hour that should snatch the veil from their faces" (42). Once again, a terror intertwined with enigma characterizes the experience of Hooper's veiled preaching. And what could his prayer mean? Does the veil merely symbolize mortality? Whatever Hooper may be trying to say, the congregation "but darkly understood him." It is particularly during the funeral that people sense Hooper to be accessing or having an eerie connection with another plane, namely, the world of the dead. Like a biblical prophet, Hooper appears able to associate with planes of existence other than human ones. A few people from the funeral offer speculations of his now being more closely connected with the world of the dead. One "superstitious old woman" declares that when Hooper leans over the body, his face exposed to it, "the corpse had slightly shuddered" (42). Though the woman in question is the only character who sees this, through her, the reader sees it too. In this subtle piece of narrating, Hawthorne lures us toward trusting a character precisely because she is unconvincingly denigrated as untrustworthy by the narrator. We come away from the passage wondering: was Hooper connecting somehow with the deceased? Additionally, if unexplained mystery lies at the center of the intended power of the veil, we could categorize the woman's "superstitious" remark as one possible response to mystery.

Another type of response is validated because it is perceived by two people. In the funeral procession, a woman fancies "'that the minister and the maiden's spirit were walking hand in hand.' 'And so had I, at the same moment,' said the other" (43). This remark, this mysterious sense of perceiving, concludes the funeral scene. Having considered the "superstitious" woman's observation, readers are now given two witnesses. The speakers are not described except that they walk among those in the funeral procession, and their words, the verbal manifestation of the effect of the minister's veil at the funeral, are given the weight of finality.

Unsettling as the responses that the mysterious veil provokes are, indeed, *because* they are unsettling, this quality lends itself to the constructive power that the veil has during Hooper's lifetime, which the narrator states outright:

> Among all its bad influences, the black veil had the one desirable effect, of making its wearer a very efficient clergyman. By the aid of his mysterious emblem—for there was no other apparent cause—he

> became a man of awful power, over souls that were
> in agony for sin. His converts always regarded him
> with a dread peculiar to themselves, affirming,
> though but figuratively, that, before he brought
> them to celestial light, they had been with him be-
> hind the black veil. Its gloom, indeed, enabled him
> to sympathize with all dark affections. (49)

It remains an unsettling truth of the narrative that whatever
can be said for the veil, its effectiveness lies in the fact that it
disturbs people. Hawthorne is careful to assert that "there
was no other apparent cause" than the "mysterious emblem"
itself; for example, Hooper does not suddenly change his
preaching style. The minister's converts, like the congregation in the opening sermon, see themselves, their own sin,
reflected in the veil. This resonates with an important aspect
of the nature of a parable: on the surface it is a story that
people can interpret in various ways, but part of the reason
for its being housed in an enigmatic form is because it is the
vehicle for a truth that cannot be fully interpreted.

Yet seeking to interpret even the ultimately unexplaina-
ble may be the duty of the religious seeker. Speaking of early
rabbinic relationships to the mysteries of Torah, Michael
Fishbane writes that "interpretation, therefore, partakes of
the sanctity of Scripture even as it further reveals it: for the
role of interpretation is neither aesthetic illumination nor
aesthetic judgment, but rather the religious duty to expound
and extend, and so to reactualize the ancient word of God
for the present hour" (*The Garments of Torah: Essays in Biblical Hermeneutics*, 38). To write or speak a parable is to ask
the audience to engage in an act of interpretation. This may
or may not be a religious act, depending on the nature of the

parable. Still, a parable is generally a religious genre, and in writing a parable, Hawthorne invites inquiry. And because Hooper's veil will never be lifted, the interpretative task can end in frustration or an embrace of mystery.

The ways in which people of Hooper's community engage in various modes of interpretation of the veil provide examples for viable responses to the mystery. Though many ultimately reject the minister, everyone in the narrative applies limits to and indulges in at least some speculation about the veil. The unsettling enigma seems to compel them to do so, to do anything to diminish (or for the devotees to heighten) the unsettling power of its mystery. From the most "sophisticated" responses to the veil to those that seek ways to distance themselves from it, the veil, like a parable, commands interpretation. The speculation that Hooper associates with the dead grows into a fable that circulates around the town "that the stare of the dead people drove him" from his late afternoon walks to the graveyard (48). This kind of attitude toward Hooper, as well as the way children avoid him, heightens his own terror of the veil: "Their instinctive dread caused him to feel, more strongly than aught else, that a preternatural horror was interwoven with the threads of the black crape" (48). The veil has a life of its own insofar as it has a marked power over Hooper, and the perception of the veil by others can affect his own perception of it. Hooper goes to great lengths to avoid seeing his own veiled reflection. He avoids mirrors and still water "lest...he should be affrighted by himself" (48). It is as though he is just another member of the community, equally horrified by the veil. And while he can feel the weight and horror of the veil, and presumably knows the terms of his wearing it—that he is bound to do so throughout his life—he does not carry on as though he lived in a state of full understanding of the veil. He is at its mercy as much as is everyone else.

When an aged Hooper nears his death, the association between the veil and other planes of existence is no less pervasive: "For some time previous, his mind had been confused, wavering doubtfully between the past and the present, and hovering forward, as it were, at intervals, into the indistinctness of the world to come" (50). The way in which the aging Hooper seems caught amid various temporal planes brings us back to biblical prophecy and the concept of the prophetic perfect tense. Even before Hooper starts to decline, a fundamentally unsettling aspect of his wearing the veil is the way in which it triggers in the viewer an uncanny sense of being perceived; it seems to throw the community, Hooper included, open to other spheres beyond the waking reality of the everyday present experience.

Ultimately, what one says about the veil cannot be divorced from how one says it, the spirit in which one responds. In "The Minister's Black Veil," Hawthorne offers us a cross-section of how different people in Hooper's community live in response to the unsettling mystery of the veil. Exploring those responses through the cautious framework of biblical hermeneutical paradigms helps us resist the temptation to draw conclusions about the mystery at the heart of the parable. For the very genre of the parable, a symbolic narrative meant to draw out speculation, has its power in its mysterious nature, in the space between it and the feelings it is intended to evoke. "Prophecy is thus a performance to incite audiences to self-reflection and action. Not only a rhetorical act, prophecy is an embodied form of symbolic action"

(Shulman, 6). For all the provocative themes and imagery of "The Minister's Black Veil," Hawthorne invites us to dwell, resisting the comfort of conclusive analysis, in the abyss of its obscurity.

What then is the value of mystery? Might it be the only viable way, for Hawthorne, to access religious awe? To live genuinely? Fishbane describes scripture in terms of its surface meanings, its "plain-sense," as "compared to several veils—or garments—of meaning leading ultimately to the Meaning of all meaning, to the preternatural divine Reality" (44). Hawthorne's text is neither sacred nor scripture. Yet his subject— the veil—is mystery, and his genre—the parable—is a genre of religious seeking.[20] Rather than asserting an authoritative voice that lays out symbolic meaning fair and square, Hawthorne is ever curious about questions of meaning and the fertility of symbols (which he explores further in *The Scarlet Letter*). True, Hooper's veil is more often associated with sin than with the kind of abyss out of which creation issues forth. And yet, it offers the Puritan community, and the community of readers, an invitation to religious and existential depths. And these depths, these unknowns, shape Hawthorne's literary mythology of America.

---

[20] The veil also aligns with Michael Broek's argument that Hawthorne's ambiguities enable his work to question rather than reinforce exceptionalism.

-4-

A Prophet for a New World:
Hester Prynne as Suffering Servant

Hester Prynne has been described as *the* female character of American literature. Harold Bloom asserts that "of all the principle female characters in our national literature, Hester Prynne is clearly the central figure" (Bloom, 1). According to Carolyn G. Heilbrun, "Hester's greatness…is allowed to assume its almost mythic proportions; it is never chiseled down to fit a conventional view of woman's limitations" (Bloom, 28). Hawthorne himself, as narrator, writes that had Hester not had a daughter, she might have been a prophetess. Indeed, Hester is often aligned with, but never becomes, an Anne Hutchinson. Bloom observes that Hawthorne "will not let her prophesy, and will not quite prophesy for her" (Bloom, 2). If Hester is a prophet, she does not match the popular depiction of a prophet as one crying out in the wilderness, because she does not cry out. Moreover, she has committed a crime that is punishable by death, wears the mark of that crime on her bosom, and serves as the representative of sin in her Boston community.

Outcast and reserved, Hester Prynne is no self-proclaimed redeemer. Yet as such she does align with striking similarities to a biblical prophetic figure: the suffering servant. Found primarily in chapters 42, 50, and 53 in the book of Isaiah, this enigmatic figure is prophetic, messianic, national, even sacrificial: "what is here affirmed of this servant of Jehovah goes infinitely beyond anything to which a prophet was ever called, or of which a man was ever capable" (Keil and Delitzsch 53:4). Most prophets speak, redeeming the people through vocal proclamation. But the suffering servant is characteristically silent. Moreover, the primary aspects of his[1] experience—such as being rejected, despised, and bearing the sins of the community—also resonate with Hester Prynne. If Hester is the first artist of the New World, could she also be its first prophet? Is there a place for a prophet in America? Yes. She, like Isaiah's servant figure, does not look like the stereotypical prophet, does not cry out, and suffers because of her community's unwarranted attacks.

Hawthorne can be seen as offering negative commentary on the origins of America if the first prophet of the New World is a woman cast out as a sinner for the crime of adultery. And yet, there seems to be a new set of rules for that wilderness. Hester is not executed for a crime, which, as the women point out in the opening scaffold scene, technically warrants stricter punishment. Hester's mild punishment can be substantiated historically: for all their stereotypical image of a stern, dour, rigid society, Puritans were surprisingly leni-

---

[1] In Isaiah's text the servant is a male figure, so I will refer to him as such in this discussion.

ent when it came to certain punishments, including adultery. Ultimately, the suffering servant tropes lead the reader to a sympathetic Hester Prynne. As suffering servant, she takes the unique position of being both the lowliest and most exalted individual in the community. She must be cast out and condemned to heal her community. Though others in the town are guilty of sin—those who blush and avert their eyes when they glance at the scarlet letter, those who Hester can sense are fellow sinners, and he who shared in Hester's sin—it is Hester who is officially labeled a sinner, and Hester who becomes Boston's comforter and counselor.

Like the suffering servant, who is a new kind of figure that will bring judgment to the nations, Hester Prynne is America's prophet. In the penultimate paragraph of the novel, the narrator speaks of her as a potential prophet figure: "Earlier in her life, Hester had vainly imagined that she herself might be the destined prophetess, but had long since recognized the impossibility that any mission of divine and mysterious truth should be confined to a woman stained with sin, bowed down with shame, or even burdened with a lifelong sorrow" (263). Hawthorne uses irony in numerous narrative contexts, and this passage is no exception. Both Dimmesdale and Hester regard their sin as detrimental to their ability to be proper spiritual leaders for the community. However, the novel shows that the individual who identifies with the lowest sinner is *best* able to empathize with and serve as a moral teacher for the community. Like Hawthorne's other prophets, Hester knows pain. But more than any of the other prophets, she embodies and dedicates her life to compassionate outreach and as such she brings about the fullest of restorations: an awaking of compassion in the hearts of her community and the reversal of their perception of her sinful nature. This reflects the prophecies about the servant in Isaiah. An exploration of the servant texts in light of *The Scarlet Letter* reveals suffering servant elements in Dimmesdale to a degree, but Hester to the fullest. These characterizations inform Hawthorne's concern with creating a historical mythology for the origins of America, and work to endear Hester to the reader. There is a place for a prophet in the New World, and Hawthorne depicts Hester as the best possible prophet available to this imperfect Puritan colony, this community founded on questionable acts of usurpation and doctrines of rigidity. This is not a love story. It is the story of a woman who bears the sins of the community, a prophet who serves as comforter and redeemer for an infant nation.

In general, Hawthorne's writings reveal a somewhat stereotypical view of biblical prophets: they possess privileged knowledge and use that knowledge to utter prophecies of future doom for the community. Though his stories may reflect this sort of traditional understanding of biblical prophecy, Hawthorne nevertheless imbues them with ambiguity—as we have just seen in "The Minister's Black Veil"—both in terms of the narrative itself and his narrative technique. References to prophecy and the characters of Dimmesdale and Hester as prophetic figures shape Hawthorne's project of creating a nuanced vision of colonial Salem.[2] The initial

---

[2] "Soon, likewise, my old native town will loom upon me through the haze of memory, a mist brooding over and around it; as if it were no portion of the real earth, but an overgrown village in cloud-land, with only imaginary inhabitants to people its wood-

mention of prophecy in "The Custom House" precedes the narrator's discovery of the scarlet letter and subsequent sense of calling to write the story: "There was always a prophetic instinct, a low whisper in my ear, that, within no long period, and whenever a new change of custom should be essential to my good, a change would come" (26). In this passage, prophecy seems to refer to foreshadowing and change. As Hawthorne begins his narrative, the term *prophecy* retains this character of future-telling, but it generally refers to negative foreshadowing. In "A Forest Walk," for example, Pearl walks along a stream that seems to be making "a prophetic lamentation about something that was yet to happen" (187). Again, we see the association of negative or wistful sentiment with a future-oriented event connected with the use of the concept of prophecy.

Hester could be said to possess any number of biblical prophetic characteristics. Like many prophets, she is singled out from her community, she serves as a community advisor, and she has knowledge of who is guilty of sin. But most prophets are vocal about their views and concerns; they are mouthpieces of God.

Somewhat like Reverend Hooper, however, Hester's service to her community involves her silence. This also reflects the Hebrew word, הסתר (*hester*), which means *hidden*. In these and other ways, Hester resembles the suffering servant depicted in the book of Isaiah. Several passages that describe the servant are Isaiah 42:1–3, 50:4–6, and 53:1–12.

---

en houses, and walk its homely lanes, and the un-picturesque prolixity of its main street" ("The Custom House," 44).

This collection of verses characterizes one who does not cry out, who brings judgment, who experiences suffering, who is rejected by the community, and who subsequently provides healing to that community.

Isaiah 42:1–3 centers on the contrast between the suffering servant's seeming impotence and his being God's chosen servant who brings justice to the earth:

> Behold my servant, whom I uphold; mine elect, in whom my soul delighteth; I have put my spirit upon him: he shall bring forth judgment to the Gentiles.[3] He shall not cry, nor lift up, nor cause his voice to be heard in the street. A bruised reed shall he not break, and the smoking flax shall he not quench: he shall bring forth judgment unto truth. (Isa. 42:1–3)

God is the speaker in these lines, stating first that this individual pleases God, that God has put God's spirit upon him, and that the servant brings justice "to the Gentiles," or, to those beyond his original community. A common understanding of this figure is that "the servant of Jehovah who is presented to us here is distinct from Israel" (Keil and Delitzsch 42:1). Yet at the same time he is representative of the nation; he "appears as the embodied idea of Israel, i.e., as its truth and reality embodied in one person" (Keil and Delitzsch 42:1). It is ironic that so great an individual appears so ineffectual on the surface. The speaker uses a series of negatives to assert that the servant will not cry out, lift up his voice, or cause his voice to be heard in the street. Moreo-

---

[3] The Hebrew term גּוֹיִם translated here as *Gentiles* means *nations*.

ver, he will not even break the likes of an already weak reed, or put out a dwindling, almost exhausted flame. Yet "he shall bring forth judgment unto truth." Far mightier than displays of strength or verbal prowess will be justice that the servant will faithfully represent and bring forth.

In Isaiah 50:4–6, the servant speaks in the first person. In this passage, the speaker's words highlight the tension between his serving as effective comforter to the weary, and one who bears the burden of abuse:

> The Lord GOD hath given me the tongue of the learned, that I should know how to speak a word in season to him that is weary: he wakeneth morning by morning, he wakeneth mine ear to hear as the learned. The Lord GOD hath opened mine ear, and I was not rebellious, neither turned away back. I gave my back to the smiters, and my cheeks to them that plucked off the hair: I hid not my face from shame and spitting. (Isa. 50:4–6)

The servant explains that God has granted him the ability to speak comfort to those who are weary, that he neither rebelled nor turned backward, and that he willingly withstood physical and psychological attacks. Verse 4 is in the present tense, suggesting that the servant's ability to "speak a word in season to him that is weary" continues to be one of his character traits. That the servant has not rebelled and not hid his face from shame and spitting reflects actions (in the negative) that are written in the past tense; they are events that have taken place that shape his present character. In the middle of the pericope is the line, "The Lord GOD hath opened mine ear." This suggests that the servant has received privileged knowledge, knowledge that might make others want to rebel or turn away. But this individual resists that temptation, and bears the full weight of what comes with this knowledge.

The longest and most well-known section of text given to the enigmatic suffering servant is in Isaiah 53. Downtrodden and rejected, the servant figure depicted is an unlikely hero. The section opens with an expression of fear that people will not believe the report of such a person. He grew up out of an improbable, unfertile setting, and he is not beautiful to look at; he does not have the physical qualities or oratory prowess one would expect of a leader (2).[4] The voice is now in the first-person plural:

> He is despised and rejected of men; a man of sorrows, and acquainted with grief: and we hid as it were our faces from him; he was despised, and we esteemed him not. Surely he hath borne our griefs, and carried our sorrows: yet we did esteem him stricken, smitten of God, and afflicted. But he was wounded for our transgressions, he was bruised for our iniquities: the chastisement of our peace was upon him; and with his stripes we are healed. All

---

[4] Of course, this is the one aspect the beautiful Hester Prynne does not share with Isaiah's unattractive suffering servant. The contrast marks a significant departure from the servant figure. Yet the degree to which this verse depicts one whose physical appearance is the opposite of what we might expect of a great leader, prophet, or messiah stands in perfect accord with Hester. Sensual, maternal, dazzlingly beautiful, Hester is not the typical image of a prophet.

we like sheep have gone astray; we have turned every one to his own way; and the LORD hath laid on
him the iniquity of us all. He was oppressed, and he
was afflicted, yet he opened not his mouth: he is
brought as a lamb to the slaughter, and as a sheep
before her shearers is dumb, so he openeth not his
mouth. (Isa. 53:3–7)

This passage offers a fuller picture of the servant. The speakers state that they treated him contemptibly, and that he endured terrible suffering. The servant bore their sins, and
through his suffering, they are healed. The speakers have
gone astray, and the servant suffers because of their sins.
Though he was oppressed and afflicted, he, like a speechless
lamb, did not voice any resistance. The passage continues to
describe the way in which the servant was taken out of prison, cut off from the living (8), and had never done violence
or spoken ill of anyone (9). Having been labeled a sinner, it
was he who bore the inequities of many, having "poured out
his soul unto death" (12). Based on this and the other servant
passages in Isaiah, three central characteristics of the servant
involve his silence: he does not speak out in the street or
against individuals; he endures attacks from a community of
sinners and in his role as intercessor; and he listens to and
bears the grief of the sinners, working on their behalf.

Two primary scholars of the suffering servant texts are
Harry M. Orlinsky and Bernd Janawski. Orlinsky argues that
the servant's suffering is not a vicarious suffering because he

is the prophet Isaiah[5] himself, suffering because of his prophetic office. Janawski underscores the paradox of the servant's predicament. Because his suffering is directly connected to his righteousness, his existence dissolves traditional correlations between actions and consequences.

In his lecture "The so-called 'Suffering Servant' in Isaiah 53," Orlinsky concludes that the individual described in Isaiah 53 does not represent the nation of Israel, as many have suggested. Neither is there any actual indication of vicarious suffering in the passage. Orlinsky asserts that the tradition of reading these verses as foreshadowing the life and death of Jesus has led to the servant-as-nation and other misreadings of Isaiah 53 (Orlinsky, 30). A primary reason that the blameless servant figure should not be read as a personification of the nation of Israel is that according to Second Isaiah,[6] Israel is far from innocent. Israel is guilty of breaking the covenant with God, and because of this sin will undergo punishment at the hand of the Babylonians. Neither here nor anywhere in Isaiah or the Hebrew Bible is there any indication that God intends an innocent Israel to suffer in order that the surrounding gentile nations may be purged from sin (9).

Numerous covenants throughout the Hebrew Bible stipulate that God will protect and develop Israel if Israel remains faithful to God. As Orlinsky explains, this sort of covenant is a legally binding contract that "assured both the obedient and the rebellious...their proper due. Nothing

---

[5] Many biblical scholars divide the book of Isaiah into three parts: chapters 1-39 make up First Isaiah, 40-55 Second (or Dutero-) Isaiah, and 56-66 Third (or Trito-) Isaiah.

could be farther from this basic concept of *quid pro quo*, or from the spirit of biblical law, or from the teachings of the prophets, than that the just and faithful should suffer vicariously for the unjust and faithless" (22). Therefore, the concept of vicariousness is one that has been read into Isaiah 53 from later, primarily Christian, generations; eisegesis has superseded exegesis (3).[7]

What should be understood from the Isaiah 53 passage is that one has suffered because of the community's transgressions (24). Orlinsky suggests that the individual who suffers is the prophet himself, Second Isaiah. The prophet suffers because it is the nature of his occupation to cry out against the sins of the people and to suffer as a result, though it is not he who is guilty of sin. Therefore, "when the people were made whole again, when their wounds were healed, it was only because the prophet had come and suffered to bring them God's message of rebuke and repentance" (26). Moreover, Orlinsky argues, the element of vicariousness is lacking because the guilty do not go unpunished. Their nation is attacked, occupied, and forced into exile. The suffering servant, then, does not deserve the capital "S" that associates him with vicariousness. For Orlinsky, he plays neither more nor less than the role other prophets, such as Jeremiah and Ezekiel, play.

Orlinsky also asserts that the characteristics of meekness and humility that have been associated with the suffering servant are unwarranted (26–27), and that hyperbole colors the servant passage: "some of the expressions are to be taken

---

[7] Hawthorne also does this to a degree.

as poetic exaggeration rather than as literal fact, [such as] the language of the suffering, and even of the death of the person involved" (29). This is supported by parallels between Isaiah 53 and lines from Jeremiah, such as "I was like a docile lamb led to the slaughter, I did not know it was against me they devised schemes," (Jer. 11:19) and so on (29). As Orlinsky states, "everyone knows Jeremiah was neither docile as a lamb nor was he slaughtered in Judah and cut off from the land of the living" (29). Finally, then, if the servant in the passage is Second Isaiah, he suffers not vicariously but *because* of the community, and hyperbole is employed to highlight the drama of his experience.

While Orlinsky looks at identity, Janowski focuses on concept. In his lecture, "He Bore Our Sins: Isaiah 53 and the Drama of Taking Another's Place," Bernd Janowski emphasizes the paradox inherent in the plight of the suffering servant (Janowski 49). Whereas a significant degree of traditional biblical logic holds that one suffers because one has been unrighteous—the perspective Job's friends assert—the suffering servant suffers *because* he *is* righteous: "Correlation of righteousness and suffering becomes plausible only in a context where traditional understandings of the relationship between actions and consequences have broken down" (Janowski 50). A new set of rules, or a lack thereof, proscribes the world in which a suffering servant figure exists, and triumphs. Thus, this world also exhibits a new concept of "success." Janowski views the suffering servant pericope to begin with the last three verses of chapter 52: 13, 14, and 15. As Janowski persuasively argues, this means that the passage begins and ends with God's words. And God speaks of the servant's ultimate triumph:

Behold, my servant shall deal prudently, he shall be exalted and extolled, and be very high. As many were astonished at thee; his visage was so marred more than any man, and his form more than the sons of men: So shall he sprinkle many nations; the kings shall shut their mouths at him: for that which had not been told them shall they see; and that which they had not heard shall they consider. (Isa. 52:13–15)

That the suffering servant story would be bookended by God's perspective is structurally logical. As Janowski argues, God's "perspective says that the Servant has not failed before Yahweh; Yahweh rather proclaims his future 'success,' as the Servant had hoped but never experienced" (61). Suffering is therefore part of God's plan for the servant, yet it is also part of a greater triumph.

The notion that outsiders perceive an individual's suffering because of the sinfulness of the individual has precedents in the psalms, "in which the suffering of the praying person appears to others as the consequence of his own guilt. Trusted friends become enemies who consistently marginalize the one they used to esteem" (63). But at a certain point, or perhaps gradually, this logic begins to break down for the community of the suffering servant. When this happens, it is also the point at which change begins to take place in the community's behavior and attitude toward the servant.

Janowski also explains why the servant is not the same as the biblical scapegoat who purges the community of sins through his "substitutionary 'atoning' death" in an area remote from the community (68): "In Isaiah 52:13–53:12 Israel's guilt is not 'gotten rid of' by a scapegoat in some remote area; it is rather endured, *borne* by the Servant" (68). Thus, the suffering servant is one who creates peace and offers comfort through remaining in the community's midst but refusing to respond to attack: "The principle that violence breeds violence exhausts itself on this one who is unconditionally ready for peace; it thus leads *ad absurdum*. This is a reality that is no longer rationally comprehensible but nevertheless exists" (72). As such, it initiates a new reality, and it marks the beginning of a national enterprise.

The analysis of Janawski and Orlinsky can inform the concept of Hester Prynne as suffering servant. Suffer though she does, Hester does not suffer vicariously; she does not purge the community of sin. Rather, she is the public face of shame and accusation, despite the fact that those around her continue to sin in private. Woman, mother, adulteress, Hester is an unexpected prophet whose unconditional compassion in the face of abuse shatters the connection between actions and consequences; her service to the community will ultimately reverse the meaning of her scarlet letter in their eyes.

Though this analysis will focus on prophetic comparisons, a biblical analysis of *The Scarlet Letter* should mention the parallels between Hester Prynne and the biblical Esther. If the self-reliant male is the Emersonian ideal of the American hero, Hester Prynne is the "supreme instance" of the American heroine (Bercovitch, *Puritan Origins*, 176). Her name of course echoes that of the biblical Esther, "homiletic exemplum of sorrow, duty, and love, and *figura* of the Virgin Mary" (Bercovitch, *Puritan Origins*, 176). Though mystery shrouds the exact motives behind Hester's life of duty and compassion for her community, she does echo Esther's striking example. Beautiful, obedient, and powerful in her wisdom of how to win the favor of the king, Esther saves her people, the Jews. In a full reversal of the evil Haman's plot, Esther ensures that Haman and those who are the enemies of the Jews are ultimately killed. Hawthorne's Hester does not have anybody killed, but she is obedient, both to the commandments she is issued and to her husband. And like Hester in Boston, Esther also "had neither father nor mother, and the maid was fair and beautiful" (Esther 2:7). Moreover, Hester remains loyal to her nation. Though it is her "sin" that roots her in American soil, and though her people initially treat her with abuse and neglect, in her loyalty to her kinsfolk, she espouses a loyalty to her nation. If Esther declares, "For how can I endure to see the evil that shall come unto my people? or how can I endure to see the destruction of my kindred?" (Esther 8:6), it could be said that Hester's refusal to speak out against her fellow Bostonians reflects a national or cultural loyalty.

In Hebrew, the name Hester derives from the word for *hidden*. In rabbinic thought, the Hebrew phrase הֶסְתֵּר פָּנִים (*hester panim*) refers to the hidden face of God (Sweeney 10 December 2009). In Greek, Hester means *star*. Bercovitch writes that Hester "is 'the hidden one' who emerges as the 'star' of the new age. The 'A' she wears expands from 'Adulteress' (we would assume, though it is never explicitly stated in Hawthorne's text) to 'Angelic.' Historically, as 'the "A" from America,' it leads forward from the Puritan 'Utopia' to that glorious destiny'" (177). Bercovitch traces a trajectory in the novel, one that moves from lowly origins to a promising future. And it is a uniquely American trajectory:

Despite Hawthorne's celebrated irony and despite his unresolved ambivalence toward the Puritan past and the democratic present, his novel yields an emphatically national design. His heroine is an intermediary prophetess, neither merely a doomed Romantic Dark Lady at her worst nor wholly a world-redeeming Romantic savior at her best, but a *figura medietatis*, like the Grey Champion "the pledge that New England's sons [and daughters] will vindicate their ancestry." (*Puritan Origins*, 177)

For Bercovitch, Hester is an "intermediary prophetess." She serves on behalf of her community and in turn on behalf of her nation, like Hawthorne's Gray Champion. Bercovitch understands Hester as an American Esther who works on behalf of her people.

Hester Prynne's public punishment initiates her service to her community. The first words spoken in the novel are those of scorn and criticism for Hester. The women of the town, "they were her country women" (50), deem the magistrates too lenient, and Hester's punishment too light. An "autumnal matron" declares, "At the very least, they should have put the brand of a hot iron on Hester Prynne's forehead. Madam Hester would have winced at that, I warrant me. But she,—the naughty baggage,—little will she care what they put upon the bodice of her gown!" Despised and rejected of her fellow countrywomen, Hester is criticized more harshly by members of her own sex than she is by men, though the youngest of the on-looking women does have some compassion for Hester: "let her cover the mark as she will, the pang of it will be always in her heart" (51).

Yet the last word is given to "the most pitiless of these self-constituted judges. 'This woman has brought shame upon us all, and ought to die'" (51–52). In opening the story with these harsh criticisms of the townswomen that end with this rigid ultimatum, Hawthorne skillfully conjures compassion for Hester. With little prior knowledge of the condemned woman, we perceive these stinging opinions as overly callous. From the beginning of the novel, Hester resembles Isaiah's suffering servant: "He is despised and rejected of men; a man of sorrows, and acquainted with grief: and we hid as it were our faces from him; he was despised, and we esteemed him not" (Isaiah 53:3). When Hester first emerges, she is despised and rejected, her silence contrasting with the critical townswomen. Moreover, the cruel words of the townswomen resonate with Orlinsky's emphasis on the sinful nature of the community for which the servant suffers.

As Hester passes through the prison door, the short walk to the scaffold seems like an eternity: "for, haughty as her demeanor was, she perchance underwent an agony from every footstep of those that thronged to see her, as if her heart had been flung into the street for them all to spurn and trample upon" (55). Hawthorne's careful phrasing does not assert, but instead suggests that she "*perchance* underwent an agony." The vivid description of this potential agony, however, carries far more weight in the reader's mind than does that little "perchance," such that the description evokes sympathy for Hester. The lines that follow these take on the odd role of softening her present agony by means of saying it will hurt more in time: "In our nature, however, there is a provision, alike marvelous and merciful, that the sufferer should never know the intensity of what he endures by its present torture, but chiefly by the pang that rankles after it" (55). The religious overtones in Hawthorne's phrase, "alike marvelous and merciful," smack of irony. He states that she does not suffer as deeply as she might, because she will suffer more in the future. Hawthorne's multi-layered diction ultimately reinforces the degree to which Hester suffers. Hester is in agony now, but, "mercifully," her sorrows will intensify as the narrative progresses. She is, past, present, and future, a woman of sorrows.

Hester's sorrow stems, in part, from her outcast status. The women in the opening scene set the tone of that status in the community. Lonely Hester dwells "without a friend on earth who dared to show himself" (81). A stereotypical Puritan rigor ensures that not one of the townspeople accepts or welcomes her. The world

> had set a mark upon her, more intolerable to a woman's heart than that which branded the brow of Cain. In all her intercourse with society, however, there was nothing that made her feel as if she belonged to it. Every gesture, every word, and even the silence of those with whom she came in contact, implied, and often expressed, that she was banished, and as much alone as if she inhabited another sphere, or communicated with the common nature by other organs and senses than the rest of human kind (84).

Hester is utterly alone, and yet she comes to make herself indispensable through her highly sought after needlework and her charitable works for the poor. Hawthorne sets her apart as almost a different species from humanity. She is not a sinner in the same rank of the biblical Cain, but she feels the pang of her exclusion deeply. Hyperbole is surely in operation here, but the allusion to Cain puts Hester's pain in biblical proportions. Though she functions within and serves her community, she is, at the same time, banished. In this way Hester does possess some characteristics of a scapegoat, who endures the sins of the community through her expulsion from the town. But more importantly, she functions as suffering servant who dwells somewhat paradoxically as one banished yet still among those who banish her. As Janowski says of Isaiah's Suffering Servant, "Israel's guilt is not 'gotten rid of' by a scapegoat in some remote area; it is rather endured, *borne* by the Servant" (68).

Hester further gains our compassion when, like the suffering servant, she is attacked by those she strives to heal: "Hester bestowed all her superfluous means in charity, on wretches less miserable than herself, and who not unfrequently insulted the hand that fed them. Much of the time, which she might readily have applied to the better efforts of her art, she employed in making coarse garments for the poor" (83). Not only does Hester persist in offering aid to those who insult her, but she resists indulging in the pleasures of her art to aid the poor. She does create spectacularly embroidered garments for the wealthy when she is commissioned to do so. But rather than giving her spare time to artistic creations for herself, Hester instead makes simple, sensible clothing for the impoverished people in her community.

Yet even the poor do not seek her out. Though Hester steadily ministers to the needy, "the poor, as we have already said, whom she sought out to be the objects of her bounty, often reviled the hand that was stretched forth to succor them. Dames of elevated rank, likewise, whose doors she entered in the way of her occupation, were accustomed to distil drops of bitterness into her heart" (84–85). The poor she strives to comfort revile her. The rich women "distil drops of bitterness into her heart." Those who might have the potential to appreciate the challenges of her situation, or at least her charitable gifts, cruelly shun her. Of the upper classes, it is particularly women that make up the community of those who actively abuse Boston's suffering servant: "they hid as it were their faces from her; she was despised, and they esteemed her not" (Isaiah 53:3).

The picture of an empowered majority denying the rights of the minority, or the one, sets the scene for martyrdom. The suffering servant has often been understood as a martyr, giving his life to the cause of his community. So too is Hester: "She was patient,—a martyr indeed,—but she forebore to pray for her enemies; lest, in spite of her forgiving aspirations, the words of the blessing should stubbornly twist themselves into a curse" (85). That Hester's patience constitutes martyrdom reflects a degree of hyperbole. As such it connects with Orlinsky's assessment of the suffering servant passages as somewhat hyperbolic: "some of the expressions are to be taken as poetic exaggeration rather than as literal fact, [such as] the language of the suffering, and even of the death of the person involved" (Orlinsky, 29). Yet the daily onslaughts she bears without cursing those that malign her is highly admirable. Moreover, if it were possible to say that she does not pray for her enemies in a way that garners respect for Hester, Hawthorne does it. The narrator does not simply say, "but she did not pray for her enemies," though, that is the implied meaning of Hawthorne's sentence. But he stealthily follows it up with a motivation even more admirable than praying for her enemies: she is so aware of her human fallibility, conscious that her prayers might twist around into something negative, that she refrains from praying for them all together. In this way, Hester surpasses Dimmesdale in humility and upright intention. He knows that each mention he makes of his own worthlessness only serves to elevate him in the eyes of his parishioners, which in turn makes him feel increasingly wretched. Hester, however, is more spiritually mature, abstaining completely from that which might make her guilty of deception.

In many ways, Hester may seem too good to be true. As the descriptions of her as martyr imply, hyperbole plays a role in creating sympathetic characterizations of both Hester and Isaiah's suffering servant. In both contexts, this literary device emphasizes the lowliness of the servant and the extremes of his or her suffering: "Continually, and in a thousand other ways, did she feel the innumerable throbs of anguish that had been so cunningly contrived for her by the undying, the ever-active sentence of the Puritan tribunal" (85). To put it mildly, Hester Prynne hurts. The novel is laden with great proportions that give the narrative a mythic cast. At the opening of the narrative, for example, Hawthorne depicts America's earliest women settlers as physically bigger than are the women of Hawthorne's time. Literally and figuratively larger than life, descriptions such as these enhance the epic quality of the story. In so doing, Hawthorne creates an appropriate background for the New World's prophet of extremes, the suffering servant.

And what could be more extreme than the idea of one officially set apart to bear the full burden of the sorrows of a community? Of a nation? In this way too, Hester echoes the suffering servant: "Surely he hath borne our griefs, and carried our sorrows: yet we did esteem him stricken, smitten of God, and afflicted" (Isaiah 53:4). In speaking from the first-person plural perspective of those who sinned against the servant, Second Isaiah prompts sympathy from the audience. Any sense of boasting or self-pity that might have arisen from the servant speaking of his own predicament dissolves in the fact that he is here honored by those who once attacked him. Assuming no responsibility for the abuse they directed toward the servant, they felt justified in attacking him because they considered him chosen by God as one who deserved punishment. But, in a complete reversal, they come to realize that he has been chosen by God to heal them. The starkness of that turnaround is as powerful for Hester as it is for Isaiah's servant. It is difficult not to be moved by the image of one who, scorned and outcast, ultimately comforts and heals her erstwhile enemies.

One of the most direct ways in which Hawthorne elicits compassion for Hester is in asking a direct question: "Had Hester sinned alone?" (86). Obviously not. Regardless of whether she could be said to bear the sins of the community, she does take the full blame for the act she shared with Dimmesdale. After the question of Dimmesdale's involvement is addressed, the issue of other sinners in the community comes to the fore. First there are those whom Hester senses as fellow sinners. Then there are those who treat her with contempt and ridicule. In her blameless behavior, despite being publicly labeled as the one and only official sinner amidst a sea of sinners, Hester gains absolution. Like Isaiah's servant, there is no deception in her; meanwhile, the rest of the community is guilty of hidden sin, and their leader, Dimmesdale, is the guiltiest of them all.

Indeed, Hester begins to believe that the mark she was given as a punishment for her own sin is giving her the ability to sense which other people in her community are likewise guilty of something. That said, Hester takes no comfort in the thought of sharing a community with fellow sinners. Her dislike of this "gift" encourages the reader to believe there is truth in her special ability:

> she felt or fancied, then, that the scarlet letter had endowed her with a new sense. She shuddered to believe, yet could not help believing, that it gave her a sympathetic knowledge of the hidden sin in other hearts....that the outward guise of purity was but a lie, and that, if truth were everywhere to be shown, a scarlet letter would blaze forth on many a bosom besides Hester Prynne's?... In all her miserable experience, there was nothing else so awful and so loathsome as this sense. (86)

Even Hester's special abilities cause her to suffer. Yet this is the plight of the prophet as suffering servant: she possesses a special calling, knowledge, and abilities, and in exercising those abilities, she suffers. As Orlinsky says of the suffering servant, this is the nature of the prophet's career.

The notion that if the truth were made visible, many other people might have scarlet letters on their bosoms echoes "The Minister's Black Veil." For Hooper, it is not so much any particular sin, as it is the mystery of the veil that isolates him from his community. At his deathbed, Hooper declares, "I look around me, and, lo! on every visage a Black Veil!" (52). Hooper speaks figuratively or perhaps literally, stating that he sees the same black veil on the faces of those around him. His special knowledge of the sins of those in his community prefigures Hester's sense that the scarlet letter gives her of the sinners in her town. We might expect Hester to find comfort in knowing others around her are guilty of sin. Perhaps she might have been concerned with bringing their sin to light as well. But "Hester Prynne yet struggled to believe that no fellow-mortal was guilty like herself" (87). Not only does she dislike the idea that others are guilty of sin, but she also struggles to believe it to be true. It is not clear whether this stems from a naïve trust in humanity, or a quality of self-deprecation. But it accords with the suffering servant's purity and her career as an ideal prophet who lives to serve others and believes in their ultimate goodness.

Yes, Hester bears and eases the griefs of the townspeople through ministering to the needs of everyone. She places her energy into aiding the sick, the poor, and the emotionally downtrodden:

> While Hester never put forward even the humblest title to share in the world's privileges...she was quick to acknowledge her sisterhood with the race of man, whenever benefits were to be conferred. None so ready as she to give of her little substance to every demand of poverty; even though the bitter-hearted pauper threw back a gibe in requital of the food brought regularly to his door, or the garments wrought for him by the fingers that could have embroidered a monarch's robe. None so self-devoted as Hester, when pestilence stalked through the town. In all seasons of calamity, indeed, whether general

or of individuals, the outcast of society at once found her place. (161)

Reaping no social benefits for herself whatsoever, Hester is the town's greatest comforter. As indispensable to her community as she is, the reader begins to wonder if the town would be in worse shape if Hester had never been accused of adultery. The ways in which she helps her fellow Bostonians outweigh the sin she committed, which hurt no one but her absent husband (though now it tortures Dimmesdale). Every aspect of Hester's relationship to the community mitigates the negative results of Hester's sin. Hawthorne has created the most sympathetic sinner possible.

Perhaps this notion of one who is treated as a sinner but treats others like saints—the paradox inherent in the existence of the suffering servant—raises the question of not just Hester's self-delusion but also that of the reader. Is the narrator tricking us into feeling sympathetic for Hester? It is more the case that we are being convinced that Hester's "sin" was not so bad after all. Though she does not assert herself as deserving recognition or fair treatment, she steadfastly asserts herself in situations where assistance is needed:

She came, not as a guest, but as a rightful inmate, into the household that was darkened by trouble; as if its gloomy twilight were a medium in which she was entitled to hold intercourse with her fellow-creatures. There glimmered the embroidered letter, with comfort in its unearthly ray. Elsewhere the token of sin, it was the taper of the sick-chamber. It had even thrown its gleam, in the sufferer's hard extremity, across the verge of time. It had showed him where to set his foot, while the light of earth was fast becoming dim, and ere the light of futurity could reach him. In such emergencies, Hester's nature showed itself warm and rich; a well-spring of human tenderness, unfailing to every real demand, and inexhaustible by the largest. Her breast, with its badge of shame, was but the softer pillow for the head that needed one. She was self-ordained a Sister of Mercy; or we may rather say, the world's heavy hand had so ordained her, when neither the world nor she looked forward to this result. The letter was the symbol of her calling. Such helpfulness was found in her,—so much power to do, and power to sympathize,—that many people refused to interpret the scarlet A by its original signification. They said that it meant Able; so strong was Hester Prynne, with a woman's strength. (161)

Though there are other sinners among the townspeople, Hester is the one who bears the public shame of sin while healing her neighbors, first physically and later emotionally as well. Similarly, through the suffering servant's anguish, others are healed: "he was wounded for our transgressions, he was bruised for our iniquities: the chastisement of our peace was upon him; and with his stripes we are healed" (Isaiah 53:5). That which sets Hester apart from the community, the embroidered "A," functions as a beacon in the darkness of the sick-chamber. The golden gleam of embroidery that once offended the townswomen as prideful, now lights the path for the sick and downtrodden. It makes Hester's bosom into a softer pillow than those that are unmarked. The one who bears openly the mark of her sin is the one who is best able to comfort. Through her compassion, Hester has utterly changed her role in the community from the despised victim of the opening scene. This shift fits Janowski's understanding of Isaiah's suffering servant narrative in which "the principle that violence breeds violence exhausts itself on this one who is unconditionally ready for peace; it thus leads *ad absurdum*. This is a reality that is no longer rationally comprehensible but nevertheless exists" (Janowski, 72). Through Hester, Hawthorne underscores the merits of an open display of one's failings, while Dimmesdale, Chillingworth, and the sinful townspeople embody the awful consequences of concealment.

Hester, however, exists as the embodiment of honesty and truth. She lives not for any joy of her own, but that others might be comforted. This is not exactly her choice. Her talk with Dimmesdale in the woods, in which she defends their relationship and suggests they leave town on the next ship, suggests that she would far prefer to have a relationship with Dimmesdale than live as an outcast who serves the needy. Nevertheless, she possesses an inexhaustible energy to comfort those in need. Hawthorne even gives her a title: Sister of Mercy. The Sisters of Mercy are Roman Catholic nuns who are dedicated to helping the poor and the sick. Their group originated in Ireland in the 1820s and spread to America in 1843. With her dedication to service and her distinctive uniform of a dress of coarse cloth and its scarlet A, Hester resembles a nun, a servant whose selfless lifestyle is committed to healing those around her.

The notion of penance is often associated with the monastic life. Hester engages in various acts of penance, such as making garments for the poor instead of works of art, and in remaining in America, the site of her sin:

> Her motive for continuing a resident of New England,—was half a truth, and half a self-delusion. Here, she said to herself, had been the scene of her guilt, and here should be the scene of her earthly punishment; and so, perchance, the torture of her daily shame would at length purge her soul, and work out another purity than that which she had lost; more saint-like, because the result of martyrdom. (80)

Because Hester suffers for the community, she is the more elevated figure. Though the narrator informs us this is half a self-delusion, it is also a half a truth. What exactly does that mean? In leaving that work to the reader, Hawthorne garners more sympathy for Hester's plight. Hester wonders if she may gain a purity more saint-like because of her "martyrdom," and Hawthorne strives to convince us that she will. Ultimately, the ambiguity enables a still more sympathetic picture of Hester as suffering servant.

Though she begins her life in New England as the representation of the worst in her community, "Hester Prynne came to have a part to perform in the world" (84). As the novel progresses, it becomes difficult to imagine the town of Boston without its suffering servant. As the prophet who appears in the time and place of greatest need, "Hester really filled a gap which must otherwise have remained vacant" (82). Her needlework, sought after by the most socially elevated citizens, is *the* fashion for the early colonial settlers. She is ever present to aid the sick and the poor. And though both the wealthy and the destitute lash out at her for her ignominy, she, like Isaiah's servant, remains silent: "He was oppressed, and he was afflicted, yet he opened not his mouth: he is brought as a lamb to the slaughter, and as a sheep before her shearers is dumb, so he openeth not his mouth" (53:7). In a novel driven by narration rather than dialogue, the hero of the story says remarkably little throughout the novel.

Our narrator describes different ways in which Hester refrains from speaking out. One area in which Hester refrains from holding forth is the public sphere: "She never battled with the public, but submitted, uncomplainingly, to its worst usage; she made no claim upon it, in requital for what she suffered; she did not weigh upon its sympathies. Then, also, the blameless purity of her life during all these years in which she had been set apart to infamy, was reckoned largely in her favor" (160). Though her constant service improves the quality of life for the entire community, she utters not a word in public settings. She is like the suffering servant who "opened not his mouth" (Isaiah 23:7), distinct from that tradition of biblical prophets who lead their communities through spoken utterances. Furthermore, in so humbly and silently accepting the punishment not only of her sin, but also of the many attacks she receives from the community members, she gains a "blameless purity."

Hester's silence pervades her life. Beyond her refusal to speak in public, she removes herself from positions in which she would have to receive expressions of gratitude. She dwells in the shadows:

> It was only the darkened house that could contain her. When sunshine came again, she was not there. Her shadow had faded across the threshold. The helpful inmate had departed, without one backward glance to gather up the meed of gratitude, if any

were in the hearts of those whom she had served so zealously. Meeting them in the street, she never raised her head to receive their greeting. If they were resolute to accost her, she laid her finger on the scarlet letter, and passed on. This might be pride, but was so like humility, that it produced all the softening influence of the latter quality on the public mind. (161–162)

Ambiguity characterizes this last remark in a way that tempts the reader to view Hester as truly humble. To simply state that she is such could fall flat and would eliminate the possibility of Hester's being prideful, which she well may be. But the primary concern here is with the public's view of Hester. Hester's respectable, servant-like actions work to convince the community of her humility, regardless of whether it can truly be said that she is or not. They who once treated her as guilty not only of adultery but also of pride now esteem her for her humility. And as much as the townsfolk exclude her from their circles, Hester also works to retain that distance. In so doing she further endears herself to them in a genuine way that contrasts with Dimmesdale's public statements of his unworthiness.

From the opening scene in which Hester is taken from prison to the scaffold, she is figuratively cut off from the land of the living. Likewise, Isaiah's servant is taken from prison and cut off from the living: "He was taken from prison and from judgment: and who shall declare his generation? for he was cut off out of the land of the living: for the transgression of my people was he stricken" (53:8). Similarly, Hester endures full and complete exclusion from the community of Boston. Even her daughter, her sole companion, is detached and antagonistic; they do not enjoy the kind of mother-daughter intimacy Hester would have liked. Pearl's exclusion from all the children's social circles reflects her mother's outcast status.

In her banishment and maltreatment, could it be said that Hester is stricken for the transgression of her people? Hester's sin of love and passion gains a quality of consecration in comparison with Chillingworth's malicious actions, Dimmesdale's hypocrisy, the townspeople's frequent rebukes, the insults of the ungrateful poor, the spiteful bitterness of the wealthy women, and her full exclusion from the community. Though legally Hester could have been killed for her crime, the magistrates reduce her punishment to three hours on the scaffold and the wearing of the A for the rest of her life. They did not stipulate that daily insults and communal rejection be a part of Hester's required punishment. Therefore, the community does transgress greatly, and as a direct result of those transgressions, Hester is stricken. The Isaiah text shows the servant as stricken through the description that, "he made his grave with the wicked, and with the rich in his death; because he had done no violence, neither was any deceit in his mouth" (53:9). The notion of making his grave with the wicked and the rich implies the servant's presumed association with the least morally upright in the community.

Though it could be argued that Hester makes her grave with the wicked insofar as she is ultimately buried next to her fellow transgressor, Dimmesdale, this line speaks more to the idea of being refused honor or special recognition at the time of death (or banishment from the community). But like the Servant, there is no deceit in Hester's mouth. She never speaks out against her punishment, never speaks out against the daily verbal onslaughts she receives from all tiers of society, never argues that she did not transgress at all, even though in her heart she seems to feel her act was not sinful, that it had "a consecration of its own" (195). In every fundamental of her character, Hester Prynne is the suffering servant of colonial Boston. And perhaps echoing the plight of the great prophet of the New Testament, Hester's return to Boston at the end of her life resonates with Jesus' statement that "it cannot be that a prophet perish out of Jerusalem" (Luke 13:33).

And what of Hawthorne's literal references to Hester as a prophet? She is twice described as almost but not quite a prophetess—first by the narrator and the second time by Hester herself. The narrator suggests that it is Pearl who holds her back from being a fully realized prophet. This perspective echoes the logic behind Catharine abandoning her gentle boy in order to prophesy on behalf of the Quakers. Hester never considers abandoning her daughter, however, so it is only in an alternate reality that Hester could be a prophetess:

> Yet, had little Pearl never come to her from the spiritual world, it might have been far otherwise. Then, she might have come down to us in history, hand in hand with Ann Hutchinson, as the foundress of a religious sect. She might, in one of her phases, have been a prophetess. She might, and not improbably would, have suffered death from the stern tribunals of the period, for attempting to undermine the foundations of the Puritan establishment. But, in the education of her child, the moth-

er's enthusiasm of thought had something to wreak itself upon. Providence,[8] in the person of this little girl, had assigned to Hester's charge the germ and blossom of womanhood, to be cherished and developed amid a host of difficulties. (165)

Because Hester's "enthusiasm of thought" has a child to focus on, she never becomes the outspoken prophetess that could have been killed after starting a religious movement. Hester possesses the natural strength of character to rebel against authority, to champion a movement, to speak out against injustice. But because she has a child, she uses that strength to stay silent, to resist defending herself from verbal attack and degradation by community members. The narrator asserts that "Providence" made Hester's job raising her daughter rather than living and dying for a prophetic cause. In contrast with Catharine who silences her maternal instincts in order to champion her Quaker cause, Hester is the

---

[8] Among Puritans, Providence was the widely accepted notion that God was actively involved in every aspect of the lives and experiences of humanity. In his discussion of Providence, David Hall cites Puritan writer Thomas Beard who asks, "Doth not every thunderclap constraine you to tremble at the blast of his voyce?' Nothing in the world occurred according to contingency or 'blind chance.' The 'all-surpassing power of God's will' was manifested in a regularity that Beard thought of as 'marvelous,' though never to be counted on completely since God retained the power to interrupt the laws of nature. The providence of God was as manifest in the unexpected or surprising as in the 'constant' order of the world" (Hall 77–78).

more admirable character for devoting herself to mothering Pearl. Though the narrator here states that she might have been a prophetess, it is the fact that she has it in her to be a prophetess that makes her admirable, not her actually taking that path. She embodies the blend of power and gentleness found in Isaiah's servant: "A bruised reed shall he not break, and the smoking flax shall he not quench: he shall bring forth judgment unto truth" (Isaiah 42:3). Hester has the capacity to found a movement, but doesn't actually do it. Yet she brings forth judgment insofar as she is a living example of compassion and service, throwing the sins of the community into relief next to her ideal example.

The second mention of Hester's potential prophet status comes in the conclusion of the novel. Hester does not suggest that her daughter held her back from being a prophet. She espouses a different view than does the narrator. Hester maintains that it is her having sinned or suffered that keeps her from being a prophet:

> Earlier in her life, Hester had vainly imagined that she herself might be the destined prophetess, but had long since recognized the impossibility that any mission of divine and mysterious truth should be confined to a woman stained with sin, bowed down with shame, or even burdened with a life-long sorrow. (263)

For Hester, the thought of being a prophet was a naïve fancy that she no longer indulges in. The narrator's criticism inherent in her "vainly" having thought she could have been a prophetess is an attack that Hester, having endured so much, does not deserve. We forgive her that youthful imagining, but would argue that her self-deception actually lies in thinking herself inadequate to the prophetic office. For it is Hester's sin that makes her so able a caregiver to her community. Her silence keeps her from being the kind that proclaims prophecies in the marketplace, but of course that makes her embody the suffering servant all the more. As a woman, a mother, a sinner, and one who has lived a life of sorrow, Hester is better able than anyone in the town to serve as prophet.

Could the New World have had a prophet that did not know suffering or sin? Would that have worked for a precarious new colony based on usurpation and in a tenuous wilderness? No, the prophet of the new world is both beyond and beneath the typical prophet crying out in such a wilderness. Hester is technically a sinner; however, the entire novel works to persuade us that her sin is not the worst of the sins in the novel, considering it renders her an invaluable comforter for every socio-economic level of the community. In a sense it is the best possible sin for the degree to which it hurts no one except a husband who may have been presumed dead, and Dimmesdale. And through this so-called sin she bears the transgressions of the community. She takes on the public burden of their sin, along with their insults and rebukes. The narrator reminds us that Hester fills a position that would have otherwise remained vacant. No one could replace her; no one else possesses the skill of needlework, which Hawthorne describes as specifically a woman's skill. By Hawthorne's logic, no man could so ably nurse both her daughter and the entire town. Dimmesdale does not. No, the fact that she is a woman, bowed down with sin, and having suffered is what makes her the ultimate prophet of the New World, the redeemer, the suffering servant.

The community's shift of opinion toward Hester completes the picture of her as Suffering Servant. Public officials were slow to forgive Hester, feeling obligated to disapprove of her because of their social rank and position. Nevertheless, their disapproval slowly wanes over the years, while regular members of the community experience a total conversion regarding their perspective on Hester:

> Individuals in private life, meanwhile, had quite forgiven Hester Prynne for her frailty; nay, more, they had begun to look upon the scarlet letter as the token, not of that one sin for which she had borne so long and dreary a penance, but of her many good deeds since. "Do you see that woman with the embroidered badge?" they would say to strangers. "It is our Hester—the town's own Hester—who is so kind to the poor, so helpful to the sick, so comfortable to the afflicted!" Then, it is true, the propensity of human nature to tell the very worst of itself, when embodied in the person of another, would constrain them to whisper the black scandal of bygone years. It was none the less a fact, however, that in the eyes of the very men who spoke thus, the scarlet letter had the effect of the cross on a nun's bosom. It imparted to the wearer a kind of sacredness, which enabled her to walk securely amid all peril. Had she fallen among thieves, it would have kept her safe. It was reported, and believed by many, that an Indian had drawn his arrow against the badge, and that the missile struck it, and fell harmless to the ground. (162–163)

The voices of those who look to Hester with respect and admiration echo those of the speakers in Isaiah 53. They had once viewed her as a wretched outcast and participated in condemning her, speaking in whispers of her public shame so many years ago. Yet now they speak boldly of her good deeds and peerless compassion. Those who had scorned her now view Hester's scarlet letter as denoting her sacred status, like "the cross on a nun's bosom." As when she is called a "Sister of Mercy," or in her decision to remain in Boston as part of her penance, reference to Hester as a monastic surfaces again. She is one whose life has been given completely in the service of others. Her sacred power has taken on a mythic quality. Legends are told of the letter serving as a shield that renders her impervious to danger. It is said that an arrow shot at her bounced off the "A" and fell, harmless, to the ground. This is the new gossip that the townspeople spread. In a total reversal of the criticism she received at the opening of the novel, Hester the suffering servant has now reached untouchable status. She is described as invincible because of her mark of sin. She is the town's greatest and most compassionate citizen. Like Janowski's suffering servant, Hester Prynne has achieved a mythic greatness through her illogical, unconditional compassion, which in turn initiates a new reality for herself and for Boston (Janowski, 72).

The redemption of those who once oppressed her is one of the servant's, and Hester's, greatest triumphs. In Hester's case it was the women of the town who were hardest on her, and it is ultimately the women for whom she serves as comforter when she returns to live out her days in Boston. Like the suffering servant, she is both pitied and revered:

But, in the lapse of the toilsome, thoughtful, and self-devoted years that made up Hester's life, the scarlet letter ceased to be a stigma which attracted the world's scorn and bitterness, and became a type of something to be sorrowed over, and looked upon with awe, yet with reverence too. And, as Hester Prynne had no selfish ends, nor lived in any measure for her own profit and enjoyment, people brought all their sorrows and perplexities, and besought her counsel, as one who had herself gone through a mighty trouble. Women, more especially—in the continually recurring trials of wounded, wasted, wronged, misplaced, or erring and sinful passion—or with the dreary burden of a heart unyielded, because unvalued and unsought came to Hester's cottage, demanding why they were so wretched, and what the remedy! Hester comforted and counselled them, as best she might. She assured them, too, of her firm belief that, at some brighter period, when the world should have grown ripe for it, in Heaven's own time, a new truth would be revealed, in order to establish the whole relation between man and woman on a surer ground of mutual happiness. (263)

In perhaps the ultimate triumph, the meaning of the scarlet letter has now completely changed for the community. No longer does it invite ridicule. It inspires admiration and awe, and for justifiable reason. Hester might have retreated in bitterness and anger from her treatment by the community—both for her public punishment for what she deemed an act of love, and the cruelty she was dealt by the individual townspeople. Instead, she speaks not a word about how she is treated but gives her life to helping others. The power of such a reversal has the effect of prompting the hearts of those who once scorned Hester to view her with a greatness of epic proportions. As such, she is the suffering servant who has a special ability to counsel the afflicted: "The Lord GOD hath given me the tongue of the learned, that I should know how to speak a word in season to him that is weary: he wakeneth morning by morning, he wakeneth mine ear to hear as the learned" (Isaiah 50:4).

Now those who once hated and rebuked Hester turn to her for consolation. Women seek advice on exactly those experiences and emotions that Hester has wrestled with, suffering from the "trials of wounded, wasted, wronged, misplaced, or erring and sinful passion—or with the dreary burden of a heart unyielded, because unvalued and unsought" (263). Having grappled with those universal sorrows only she was accused of, Hester is the sole individual through whose stripes they can be healed. Hester even suffers the pain of a heart unsought by he whose public shame she bore for them both. Despite all she has undergone, Hester not only offers consolation to those who seek her aid, she, prophet-like, inspires her people with the hope of a beautiful vision of restoration: the restoration of a relationship between men and women, founded on mutual happiness. This is an inspired vision indeed, considering both she and Dimmesdale endured a relationship of mutual misery.

And what of Dimmesdale? Is he not also a suffering servant? Like Hester, he is weighed down with emotional pain throughout the novel. As Dimmesdale withers under the burden of his sin, the townspeople only admire him more for his semblance of piety. Dimmesdale's "more fervent admirers" view him "as little less than a heavenly-ordained apostle, destined, should he live and labor for the ordinary term of life, to do as great deeds for the now feeble New England Church, as the early Fathers had achieved for the infancy of the Christian faith" (120). Dimmesdale's community singles him out as the most respected of spiritual leaders, and as he begins to grow pale and decline physically, some of his followers maintain "that the world was not worthy to be any longer trodden by his feet" (120). Moreover, as the minister of the town, he is the most likely candidate for the job of town prophet. Except he cannot fill the shoes of the Suffering Servant. Dimmesdale's obsession with his own guilt hinders his ability to serve his community. He shares the gentleness of Isaiah's servant who would not break a bruised reed, but not his ability to bring forth judgment unto truth (Isaiah 42:3).

Hawthorne does draw comparisons between Dimmesdale and biblical prophets that highlight his *potential* to be a prophetic voice for Boston. Had he not been weighed down by his conscience, his hypocrisy, (and by Chillingworth), he could have been a powerful prophetic force. We see a burst of that power at the end of the novel, described with an uncommon, overt invocation of the biblical prophets. As Dimmesdale's election sermon concludes, "a spirit as of prophecy had come upon him, constraining him to his purpose as mightily as the old prophets of Israel were constrained; only with this difference, that, whereas the Jewish seers had denounced judgments and ruin on their country, it was his mission to foretell a high and glorious destiny for the newly gathered people of the Lord" (249). Despite the positive and as such un-biblical aspect of his preaching according to our narrator, the passage goes on to imbue Dimmesdale with a "deep, sad undertone of pathos." Hawthorne's definition of prophecy generally referring to negative foreshadow is reinforced here. Yet like Hester, Dimmesdale offers up an inspiring vision of restoration for his people. Had he been strong enough to live after his great confession and to continue to offer his people hope and inspiration, he might have become a prophet extraordinaire.

For Dimmesdale is depicted as prophet-like on more than one occasion. Hawthorne's description of the power Dimmesdale has over his congregation emphasizes mystery, the mystery of both the prophet's connection with God and the effect he has on the people: "The people knew not the power that moved them thus. They deemed the young clergyman a miracle of holiness. They fancied him the mouthpiece of Heaven's messages of wisdom, and rebuke, and love" (142). As the mouthpieces of God, biblical prophets strive to communicate God's messages. The people believe God is speaking through Dimmesdale. He is seen by many in his community as a representation of God on earth: "In their eyes, the very ground on which he trod was sanctified" (142). From the perspective of his congregation, Dimmesdale takes on an unearthly holiness.

Dimmesdale grows in popularity and respect in his community as he grows weaker physically and ever more troubled emotionally. Like the suffering servant, Dimmesdale's suffering does enable him to identify more closely with the suffering of others. His own burden "gave him sympathies so intimate with the sinful brotherhood of mankind; so that his heart vibrated in unison with theirs, and received their pain into itself, and sent its own throb of pain through

a thousand other hearts, in gushes of sad, persuasive elo-
quence. Oftenest persuasive, but sometimes terrible!" (142).
Dimmesdale's personal anguish enables him to sympathize
with those around him who suffer. However, we are not giv-
en any direct sense that he effectively comforts them in any
way, that "through his stripes they are healed." They revere
him. Young women admire him. But we hear no descriptions of his selfless service in the sick-chamber or giving his
free time to helping the poor. No, it is Hester who is attend-
ing Governor Winthrop at his deathbed, while Dimmesdale
is up on the scaffold at midnight, wrestling with his conscience. The minister should have been there, not the town
sinner. But as Janowski reminds us, traditional structures
break down in the world of the suffering servant. Hester
channels her penance into serving others while Dimmesdale
beats himself up.[9] And he only grows weaker through indulging in his obsession with his soul, less and less able to
effectively minister his community, until he finally dies.

Hester is the true minister of Boston. She gives herself
in selfless service to the poor, the sick, and the afflicted.
While Dimmesdale is greatly esteemed by his parishioners,
he is too preoccupied with the weight of his sin to serve the
community. Michael Broek explains this in terms of their
ability to accept their isolation:

---

[9] An understanding of Hawthorne's own social views may offer insight into Dimmesdale's. "Acutely aware of social evils,
[Hawthorne] believed in a duty to improve even the best society,
and he knew too that decorum, prudence, and respect for conven-
tion may only be a mask for moral cowardice; a retreat, like Dimmesdale's, from the burdens of judgment" (McWilliams 313).

> The characters imagined by Hawthorne and Melville come to terms with their aloneness—whether this aloneness takes the form of a physical separation or isolation, or a spiritual and psychological one—while rejecting themselves as exceptional. Hester finally lives her life outside of the symbol system that has condemned her, transforming her "A" into "Able," but Dimmesdale, who as a Puritan minister is a representative of all that is exceptional, is dead. He cannot transcend the monologism that is his inheritance. (Broek, 10)

Well intentioned though Dimmesdale may be, Hester is the hero of the novel, not Dimmesdale. And because she "comes to terms with her aloneness" by directing her attention outward toward her community, she transcends it. Dimmesdale's aloneness, however, grows ever more inward until it implodes. F. O. Matthiessen remarks that "Dimmesdale, in his indecisive waverings, filled as he is with penance but no penitence, remains in touch with reality only in proportion to his anguish. The slower, richer movement of Hester is harder to characterize in a sentence" (*American Renaissance: Art and Expression in the Age of Emerson and Whitman*, 276). Agreed. She endures onslaught and attack whilst abstaining from speaking out in public. She endures banishment followed by acceptance. Meanwhile, as the town minister who gives sermons on Sundays and holidays, Dimmesdale could be a prophet, but he—consumed by his guilt—fails.

In many ways Hester Prynne, the suffering servant prophet of the New World, lives a life that reflects the ideal as set out in Winthrop's City on a Hill sermon, "A Model of Christian Charity"—because all eyes of the world are upon her, she exists as the example of charity, of tenderness, of maternal constancy and affection. Using irony and at times ambiguous language, Hawthorne communicates the sincerity of Hester's penitence, her strivings toward expiating her sin, and her devoted, selfless service to her community. Just as we learn of the Servant through third-person praise, Hester's magnificence couldn't be fully communicated with straightforward diction. Hawthorne imbues Hester with an epic blend of the lowly and the great. Through her full understanding of suffering and her life of unconditional compassion, she effects a felt restoration greater than any of Hawthorne's other prophets. She is the revolutionary prophet of the New World: America's suffering servant.

–5–

Prophecy and Restoration in
The House of the Seven Gables

The biblical prophetic concepts of inherited sin, the name of Hepzibah, and the folly of creating a dynasty shape *The House of the Seven Gables*. Hawthorne describes his tale as "a history of retribution, for the sin of long ago" (41). As it is in the Bible, Hawthorne's study of generational inheritance is complex. The Puritan prophet of *The House of the Seven Gables* dies in the opening scene: Matthew Maule's curse lays the foundation of the story as well as the house. This novel does not feature an individual prophet so much as it is driven by several kinds of prophetic themes. Yet a few of the characters operate as prophets during key moments in the development of those themes. Holgrave makes prophetic declarations about abolishing the past, and he has the capacity for mesmerism. Clifford enters an ecstatic state on the train as he holds forth about transcending temporal cycles. Hepzibah speaks on behalf of God's merciful nature and prays to God on behalf of her people. Uncle Venner dresses in motley

clothes and maintains an ability to live in harmonious relationship with past, present, and future.[1] While none of these
characters is a developed prophet figure, each of them displays compassionate and prophetic characteristics during
climactic scenes that forward restoration and undo the curse.
With *The House of the Seven Gables*, Hawthorne has constructed a new form of prophetic fiction.

It is Maule's prophetic utterance that undergirds the
narrative. Hawthorne's novel, however, is not about deter-
mining whether the curse *is* real. The prophecy was spoken,
and it affects both the Maule and the Pyncheon families
through the generations; thus, it is "real." And thus the biblical theme of the sins of one generation bringing disaster on
subsequent generations shapes, indeed is the official moral
of, this text. Robert Spiller sees Hawthorne's interest in inherited sin as reflecting Hawthorne's concern with America's
Puritan foundations:

> Hawthorne lived at a time when the foundations of
> that stability were being undermined, when its
> dogmas and its practices were being questioned; and
> he pulled away some of the underpinning himself.
> He felt that his generation had built its house over
> an unquiet grave—that the very qualities of iron will
> and certain faith which his ancestors believed to be
> virtues, were in reality vices, now living as ghosts to
> torment their children's children. The sense of in-

---

[1] Max Loges suggests that Uncle Venner is "a prophet-like
character" for his faith, which proves to be justified, in a brighter
future for Hepzibah: "Something still better will turn up for you.
I'm sure of it" ("Hawthorne's *The House of the Seven Gables*, 64).

herited sin, either that of commission or that attendant upon intolerance, is the keynote of the best
of Hawthorne's writings. (650)

It is no surprise that a nineteenth-century writer who returns
again and again to Puritan themes might be absorbed by the
notion of inherited sin. Hawthorne had uncomfortable feelings about a nation born in blood, and about his ancestors'
involvement in executing women for witchcraft or whipping
Quakers through the streets. While I do not unilaterally assert that *Seven Gables* reflects Hawthorne's efforts to come to
terms with his own family's past, he does engage in a productive exploration of the issues surrounding inherited sin.

The concept of the prophetic perfect tense, as discussed
in connection with "The Minister's Black Veil," can be used
to project what might happen in the future. It can also represent a kind of eternal present. It is the tense or time frame in
which past and future either collide or dissolve. Operating
out of the prophetic perfect enables moments of lucidity for
Clifford, Holgrave, Hepzibah, and Uncle Venner, which in
turn prompt some restoration of the curse's negative impact.
Uncle Venner seems to live in a steady state of appreciation,
and in that sense, he is the most consistent living prophet,
offering positive present and future-oriented statements, all
of which prove true. For Holgrave, Hepzibah, and Clifford,
it is during moments of new relationship with time that they
offer their own prophetic utterances. Driven by these prophetic moments, *The House of the Seven Gables* is a study of
the limits and possibilities of transcending inherited sin.

Before beginning an analysis of *The House of the Seven
Gables* and prophecy, we turn to biblical texts that address
inherited sin, the name of Hepzibah, and the folly of estab-

lishing a dynasty. Narratives that treat the issue of inherited family sin abound in 1 and 2 Kings. These two books make up a narrative history "that is especially concerned to explain why the people of Israel and Judah were attacked and exiled from their land in order to provide a firm theological foundation for returning to the land and rebuilding their life there in the aftermath of the exile" (Sweeney, *I & II Kings*, 1). Broadly speaking, 1 Kings depicts the sinful actions (namely, faithlessness to God through worshiping local idols) of Solomon and the kings of the Northern kingdom starting with Jeroboam ben Nebat. After Jeroboam ben Nebat instigates a pattern of sinful behavior,[2] the prophet Elijah emerges, performs miraculous works, and strives to convince kings of Northern Israel such as Ahab to restore their faith in YHWH

---

[2] According to the Deuteronomist—the individual or school of editors Bible scholars commonly credit with the final composition of the books of Joshua through 2 Kings—Jeroboam predicts that if the people worship at the temple in Jerusalem, their loyalty will be with the Judean king, Reheboam, and that Jeroboam will subsequently be killed. Therefore he sins through directing his people to keep away from the temple where they should rightfully be worshiping and instead to worship idols at local high places in the north: "If this people go up to do sacrifice in the house of the LORD at Jerusalem, then shall the heart of this people turn again unto their lord, even unto Rehoboam king of Judah, and they shall kill me, and go again to Rehoboam king of Judah. Whereupon the king took counsel, and made two calves of gold, and said unto them, It is too much for you to go up to Jerusalem: behold thy gods, O Israel, which brought thee up out of the land of Egypt" (1 Kings 12:27–28).

See Sweeney, *I & II Kings 1-44*.

and to engage in appropriate worship practices that reflect that faith. Ultimately, however, Jeroboam's sinful inheritance prevails, and Israel falls at the hand of Assyria. Descendants of Jeroboam, such as his son Nadab, are frequently described thus: "And he did evil in the sight of the LORD, and walked in the way of his father, and in his sin wherewith he made Israel to sin" (1 Kings 15:26).[3] Or later in 2 Kings: "For the children of Israel walked in all the sins of Jeroboam which he did; they departed not from them; Until the LORD removed Israel out of his sight, as he had said by all his servants the prophets" (2 Kings 17:22-23).[4] The Deuteronomist asserts that their sin justifies their family's and their descendants' ultimate loss of land.

A similar pattern unfolds in the southern kingdom of Judah after Israel has fallen. A line of sinful kings paves the way for the Babylonian takeover because they disobey God by worshipping idols instead of God. King Manasseh (whose

----

[3] These lines resonate with the Deuteronimist's regular "practice of condemning all of the northern monarchs for prompting Israel to sin. Such an agenda clearly serves the Josian [Deuteronomist], which emphasizes the condemnation of northern Israel for following in the sins of Jeroboam" (Sweeney, *I & II Kings*, 196).

[4] Once again, the Deuteronomist condemns "Israel's rebelliousness in rejecting the house of David in favor of Jeroboam (1 Kgs 11-14). Jeroboam's apostasy emerges as the basis for Israel's sins against YHWH, although the rejection of the house of David points to a political dimension as well" (Sweeney, *I & II Kings*, 395).

mother's name is Hephzibah[5]) and King Ahab are among the greatest sinners. Again, the ownership of land is central to this narrative (as it is in *Seven Gables*). In response to Manasseh's actions God declares,

> Neither will I make the feet of Israel move any more out of the land which I gave their fathers; only if they will observe to do according to all that I have commanded them, and according to all the law that my servant Moses commanded them. But they hearkened not: and Manasseh seduced them to do more evil than did the nations whom the LORD destroyed before the children of Israel. (2 Kings 21:18–19)

God is described as wanting nothing more than to allow the Israelites to stay in their land if they will hold up their end of the covenant by remaining faithful to God. But Manasseh leads the people astray, sheds innocent blood (2 Kings 21:16), and his descendants inherit both the punishment and the inclination to sin.

Yet, according to the narratives in 1 and 2 Kings, there is some hope for restoration in the reign and actions of King Josiah. A descendant of the righteous King David, Josiah, "walked in all the way of David his father, and turned not

---

[5] Nothing else is said here of Hephzibah, except that she is mother of Manasseh. One possible connection with Hawthorne's character may simply be that she is part of a sinful family line. The second reference to Hephzibah, that in Isaiah, will be discussed later in this chapter.

aside to the right hand or to the left" (2 Kings 22:2).[6] Thus one from within Jerusalem, descended from the original great king of the united kingdom of Israel, cleanses and restores the temple, "the house of the Lord" (2 Kings 22:5), and reads from the Torah.[7] In 2 Kings 23:15–18, Josiah destroys the Beth El sanctuary that had been established by Jeroboam ben Nebat in 1 Kings 12:25–13:34 (Sweeney, *I & II Kings*, 441). (Hawthorne's Clifford and Phoebe play roles similar to Josiah's in some ways.) Unfortunately, the previous kings did too much damage; Josiah's reform movement is not enough to spare Jerusalem. The prophetess Hulda's oracle "acknowledges Josiah's righteousness, but states that it cannot reverse YHWH's decree of destruction for Jerusalem be-

---

[6] This praise of turning neither to the right nor to the left is not used to describe any Judean king except Josiah. It is often found in Moses' commands to the people, and is said of Moses' successor, Joshua. The description thus "indicates that Josiah surpasses all of the monarchs of the Davidic line in his righteousness, and that he is to be compared to Joshua, Deuteronomy's ideal king, and to the Deuteronomic ideal of observance of YHWH's Torah" (Sweeney, *I & II Kings*, 441).

[7] This account of Josiah aids "in explaining the destruction of Jerusalem and the Babylonian exile. It thereby serves as a form of theodicy in that it attempts to defend YHWH's righteousness by placing the blame for the destruction of the city on the people of Judah themselves..., despite the obvious righteousness of King Josiah. The importance of such an attempt is apparent when one considers that Judah's and Jerusalem's foundational theology emphasizes YHWH's role as unconditional and absolute author of creation and guarantor of the security of the city of Jerusalem and the ruling house of David." (Sweeney, *I & II Kings*, 440)

cause of the people's apostasy. Hulda indicates that Josiah's righteousness earned him the right to a peaceful death before the catastrophe strikes" (Sweeney, *I & II Kings*, 439). Josiah's humility prompts God's compassion:

> Because thine heart was tender, and thou hast humbled thyself before the LORD, when thou heardest what I spake against this place, and against the inhabitants thereof, that they should become a desolation and a curse, and hast rent thy clothes, and wept before me; I also have heard thee, saith the LORD. Behold therefore, I will gather thee unto thy fathers, and thou shalt be gathered into thy grave in peace; and thine eyes shall not see all the evil which I will bring upon this place. (2 Kings 22: 19–20)

While the land and the house of God will be taken away from the people, he who brought about a degree of restoration, whose heart was tender, will be treated with mercy.[8]

---

[8] "Josiah's early death is presented as an act of mercy by YHWH in recognition of his unimpeachable character, but it points to the difficulties faced by the writers of this narrative who were compelled to rethink the classical Zion theology in relation to the Babylonian exile. Ultimately, the attempt to wrestle with the theological contradictions posed by the exile forced a rethinking of the notion of repentance as well. The problem is accentuated by the fact that the Chronicler presents a very different understanding of this event... [in which] Josiah emerges as the recalcitrant figure, who brings about his own death by his refusal to obey YHWH. The Chronicler thereby avoids the theological

Yet, perspectives vary on the righteousness of kings in different biblical texts. Though 1 and 2 Kings are more commonly read, and likely what Hawthorne was most familiar with, Chronicles offers contrasting views, for example, on the implications of Josiah's death. In the Deutronomist's (2 Kings) account, Josiah's peaceful death is a fulfillment of the prophetess Hulda's words that he would die in peace, though Judah will still fall as a result of the sinfulness of Manasseh. Inherited sin is central to the Deuteronomist's concern with justifying the fall of Israel and Judah. The Chronicler is concerned with understanding these catastrophes as well; however, 1 and 2 Chronicles reflect a revision of the concept of inherited sin in which everyone is responsible for their own actions. With regard to Josiah's death, the Chronicler indicates that he did not die a peaceful death but was killed in battle as a result of "his refusal to heed the word of G-d as spoken by Pharaoh Necho of Egypt. In keeping with the Chronicler's perspective, Josiah dies because of his own wrongdoing" (Sweeney, *The Prophetic Literature*, 80).

To return to the name of Hephzibah, it appears in the Hebrew Bible in two places: 2 Kings 21:1, where she is listed as the mother of Manasseh, and Isaiah 62:4 in which Jerusalem is called Hephzibah. She prefigures Hawthorne's Hephzibah in that she is connected to the family line that brings destruction on the house of Israel. The name here derives from the Hebrew verb חָפֵץ (*hapetz*), which can mean to desire, to delight in, to keep, or to take care. But perhaps the

---

and moral problems of the Kings narrative." (Sweeney, *I & II Kings*, 440)

more commonly known use of the name Hephzibah is that in Isaiah 62:4. This passage is a vision of future restoration in which Jerusalem will be called *Hephzibah*, rather than *forsaken*, because God's "delight is in her":

> For Zion's sake will I not hold my peace, and for Jerusalem's sake I will not rest, until the righteousness thereof go forth as brightness, and the salvation thereof as a lamp that burneth. And the Gentiles shall see thy righteousness, and all kings thy glory: and thou shalt be called by a new name, which the mouth of the LORD shall name. Thou shalt also be a crown of glory in the hand of the LORD, and a royal diadem in the hand of thy God. Thou shalt no more be termed Forsaken; neither shall thy land any more be termed Desolate: but thou shalt be called Hephzi-bah, and thy land Beulah: for the LORD delighteth in thee, and thy land shall be married. For as a young man marrieth a virgin, so shall thy sons marry thee: and as the bridegroom rejoiceth over the bride, so shall thy God rejoice over thee. (Isa. 62:1–5)

In this context, Hephzibah is a name that foreshadows restoration. The passage opens with Jerusalem is in the midst of difficult times. God displays God's loyalty to the city, stating that God will not rest until Jerusalem's righteousness is realized. This glorious time will be marked by God giving Jerusalem a new title. As opposed to the disparaging titles Jerusalem has lately been termed because of her transgressions (*Forsaken* and *Desolate*), she will be newly re-named *Hephzibah* because God delights in her. No longer the common prophetic image of the unfaithful bride, this picture of restoration is marked with depictions of faithful partnership. To turn to the novel under discussion, Hawthorne's Hephzibah reflects both the mother of Manasseh in 2 Kings for her association with the sinful family line, and the idea of restoration presented in the Isaian prophecy for her faithful words and deeds that lead to restoration for her family.

In a short study on Hepzibah's name and its origins in the Hebrew Bible, Max Loges argues that "there is a comical contrast between the meaning of the name 'Hepzibah' and the odd maid who bears it" (64). Citing Isaiah's definition for the name, "my delight is in her," Loges remarks that "Hawthorne's character, however, is anything but delightful and is known far and wide for her perpetual scowl, which frightens children and irritates adults" (64). No, Hepzibah is not delightful, but that is not exactly what the biblical definition implies: it says that *God* delights in her, and in the city that has once been forsaken and will soon be cause to rejoice again. Loges later moves away from Hepzibah as a comical name and addresses the degree to which its meaning reflects the shift in her position from forsaken at the beginning of the novel to the restoration she helps to bring about and finally enjoys at the end. In the passage in Isaiah, Jerusalem "is a forsaken wasteland waiting for the return of her captives. The prophet expresses faith that God will make Jerusalem's future much brighter than her present. At the beginning of *The House of the Seven Gables*, Hawthorne's Hepzibah, like Jerusalem, is described as forsaken and desolate" (65). Like the city of Jerusalem, Hepzibah's circumstances will undergo positive change, both in her own experience, and in her status as perceived by others, evinced by the neighbors commenting on the disappearing carriage near the end of the novel (66). Loges also connects the imagery of marriage in the Isaiah pericope with the marriage of Holgrave and Phoebe: "Like Jerusalem's, Hepzibah's land also will be married. The biblical passage intimates that the city will once again be populated by young people and that children will play in her streets…. No longer will [Hepzibah] live forsaken and alone in a house populated by more ghosts than warm bodies" (66). The restoration indicated by Hepzibah's name rightly involves this quality of partnership and fecundity suggested by the marriage metaphor. Interestingly, this passage from Isaiah also dissolves the concept of inheritance: though Jerusalem has once been forsaken, all of that will soon be forgotten, and God will not only forgive Jerusalem's past wrongs; God will *delight* in her.

The notion of inheritance is frequently under revision in prophetic texts. On several occasions, it is presented as an old proverb that is being reevaluated, as in these lines from Ezekiel: "What mean ye, that ye use this proverb concerning the land of Israel, saying, The fathers have eaten sour grapes, and the children's teeth are set on edge? As I live, saith the Lord GOD, ye shall not have occasion any more to use this proverb in Israel" (18:2–3). The prophetic text as we have it reflects the concern of a community moving away from the concept of inheriting the sin of a previous generation. Rather, as Ezekiel has it, "all souls are [God's]" and each person will be punished according to his or her own behavior. Yet the presence of the passage in the text speaks to the probability that the notion of generational inheritance persisted and was debated among the people for centuries.

One final text that offers possible source material for *Seven Gables* is 1 Samuel 8, in which God through the prophet Samuel elaborates on Israel's catastrophic decision to have a monarchy in the first place. Though the prophet warns that the people need no ruler beside God, they insist on a king, and so begins, it could be argued, the ultimate downfall of the nation. Samuel explains that such a ruler will greedily usurp the land and the lives of the people in it:

> And he said, This will be the manner of the king that shall reign over you: He will take your sons, and appoint them for himself, for his chariots, and to be his horsemen; and some shall run before his chariots. And he will appoint him captains over thousands, and captains over fifties; and will set them to ear his ground, and to reap his harvest, and to make his instruments of war, and instruments of his chariots. And he will take your daughters to be confectionaries, and to be cooks, and to be bakers. And he will take your fields, and your vineyards, and your oliveyards, even the best of them, and give them to his servants. And he will take the tenth of your seed, and of your vineyards, and give to his officers, and to his servants... (1 Sam. 8:11–15)

If Israel demands a king, she will be sucked dry by such a ruler. And it comes to pass that Solomon's exploits will ultimately lead to the division of the kingdom, and thenceforward will follow a line of primarily sinful kings, according to the Deuteronomistic author. Thus, Samuel warns the Israelites that if they insist on a king, they can soon expect to be oppressed. This resonates with *Seven Gables* insofar as the Puritan progenitor, Colonel Pyncheon, is essentially trying to set up a dynasty. He takes the rightful land of others, establishes a tradition of oppression against the violated Maules, and for all intents and purposes crowns himself king. The biblical precedent for this behavior in the prophetic writings of Samuel foreshadow the same conclusion as do Hawthorne's writings: the usurping monarchy, established in a land that had no need for a king, will ultimately crumble.

Like the biblical narrators, Hawthorne describes his tale as "a history of retribution, for the sin of long ago" (41). After laying out the moral of the story in the preface, then asserting that morals more often hinder than enhance novels, Hawthorne proceeds to open the narrative proper with it:

> Hence too might be drawn a weighty lesson from the little regarded truth, that the act of the passing generation is the germ which may and must produce good or evil fruit, in a far distant time; that, together with the seed of the merely temporary crop, which mortals term expediency, they inevitably sow the acorns of a more enduring growth, which may darkly overshadow their posterity. (6)

While the preface gives us permission to disregard the moral, here it is again, front and center, driving the narrative. In this way *Seven Gables* echoes the prophetic narratives of 1 and 2 Kings, which are steadily driven by the concept of inherited sin, as well as inherited blessing. Various kings, such as Manasseh (Hepzibah's son) and Jeroboam initiate and perpetuate the sins of their royal line. Those who are righteous in the eyes of the Deuteronomist, such as Josiah, are said to follow in the line of King David.

Hawthorne states that the awful nature of the death of Matthew Maule "made it seem almost a religious act to drive the plough over the little area of his habitation, and obliterate his place and memory from among men" (7). The narrator describes the near "religious act" with biblical tones and diction that echo the King James translation: the "area of his habitation" and the poetic absoluteness of "obliterat[ing] his place and memory from among men" (7) evoke a grand style typical of biblical narratives. In speaking of his ruin before speaking of his "crime," Hawthorne conjures sympathy for Maule before stating that he "was executed for the crime of witchcraft" (7). He is thus presented as innocent of this crime, and justified in uttering the curse that shapes the novel. A moment before he is about to be executed,

> Maule had addressed [Pyncheon] from the scaffold, and uttered a prophecy, of which history, as well as fireside tradition, has preserved the very words.— "God," said the dying man, pointing his finger with a ghastly look at the undismayed countenance of his enemy, "God will give him blood to drink!" (8)

This, Hawthorne declares, is a prophecy, the words of which are validated by two camps: "history" and "fireside tradition." Though these sources are vague, that two sources concur about Maule's prophecy lends it authority. Of course, the striking image the narrator paints of the dying man, harness about his neck, stretching out his pointed finger "with a ghastly look at the undismayed countenance of his enemy," likewise ingrains the incident in the minds of the reader.

But now to the prophetic utterance itself. "God will give him blood to drink!" cries Matthew Maule before he is executed. The most immediate biblical allusion here is to the Book of Revelation in the New Testament. In Revelation 16:6, after speaking of the punishment of the wicked, the speaker states, "For they have shed the blood of saints and prophets, and thou hast given them blood to drink; for they are worthy." The word *worthy* indicates that the wicked deserve their punishment. Hawthorne also refers to this line from Revelation in "The Gentle Boy" when Catharine is uttering her own prophetic oracle: "Woe to them that shed the blood of saints!" (82). In "The Gentle Boy" and *Seven Gables*, these prophetic utterances alluding to the line from Revelation bring the past, present, and future together with a sudden awfulness.

Besides the inheritance of the curse itself, the Pyncheon descendants seem to inherit Colonel Pyncheon's "hard, keen sense, and practical energy....His character, indeed, might be traced all the way down, as distinctly as if the Colonel himself, a little diluted, had been gifted with a sort of intermittent immortality on earth" (19). The twofold nature of inheritance comes forth through these traits in the Pyncheon family. That the original Colonel lives on in each generation of his descendants may be something to be proud of when they embody his assertive characteristics, but it becomes unsettling when they inherit a negative conscience: "For various reasons, however, and from impressions often too vaguely founded to be put on paper, the writer cherishes the belief that many, if not most, of the successive proprietors of this estate, were troubled with doubts as to their moral right to hold it" (20). Along with his strengths, the Colonel's descendants inherit the influence of Maule's curse.

True, the Pyncheons legally own the house and the land it sits upon,

> but old Matthew Maule, it is to be feared, trode downward from his own age to a far later one, planting a heavy footstep, all the way, on the conscience of a Pyncheon. If so, we are left to dispose of the awful query, whether each inheritor of the property—conscious of wrong and failing to rectify it—did not commit anew the great guilt of his ancestor, and incur all its original responsibilities. And supposing such to be the case would it not be a far truer mode of expression to say, of the Pyncheon family, that they inherited a great misfortune, than the reverse? (20)

Maule's curse has continued to weigh on the usurping Pyncheon family throughout the generations. The impression that the Pyncheons inherited both the fortitude of Colonel Pyncheon, and the weight of the curse Maule laid upon him, prompts a challenging question: if generations of Pyncheons are conscious of their ancestor's wrongdoing, are they also guilty of not striving to rectify past wrongs? If this is the case, then Maule's curse, brought on by the wrongful usurpation of Maule's land and the murder of the man himself, is a heavier inheritance than that of the grand house of Seven Gables. What does seem to be the case is that those over the generations who are not "conscious of wrong" commit the greatest sins. Oblivious to the cruelty of his greed, Judge Pyncheon serves as the prime example of this. In the biblical context of 1 and 2 Kings, those rulers who persist in following in the footsteps of the sinful kings before them are viewed as continuing to commit the crimes of their predecessors. Yet those who are aware of their ancestors' sins and strive to reverse the pattern, such as Josiah in 2 Kings, and tenderhearted Hepzibah in *Seven Gables*, are the great heroes of their narratives.

Maule's prophecy influences both the Pyncheon family and the townspeople in irreversible ways. Though it was directed at Colonel Pyncheon, the curse becomes intergenerational, growing in its influence and legendary status. As that which is open to speculation, anything that could be tangentially perceived as connected with the curse is taken as such by many in the family and the community at large. Most obvious is the case that Colonel Pyncheon dies in a sudden and mysterious way, sitting up at his desk, with blood on his collar. Hawthorne offers a hazy web of rumors that various people put forward as having potentially caused the death, such as a murderer slipping in through the window, or a skeleton hand "seen at the Colonel's throat" (16). Yet none of these rumors lessen the connection between the prophecy and the death. Interestingly, they may strike the reader as more speculative, less credible than the curse uttered by a wrongfully executed man. Once spoken, the community cannot let go of it. After the Colonel's death,

> the popular imagination, indeed, long kept itself busy with the affair of the old Puritan Pyncheon and the wizard Maule; the curse, which the latter flung from his scaffold, was remembered, with the very important addition, that it had become a part of the Pyncheon inheritance. If one of the family did but gurgle in his throat, a bystander would be likely enough to whisper, between jest and earnest—"He has Maule's blood to drink!"—The sud-

den death of a Pyncheon, about a hundred years ago, with circumstances very similar to what have been related of the Colonel's exit, was held as giving additional probability to the received opinion on this topic. (21)

The sudden death of a descendent of "the old Puritan Pyncheon" lends the prophecy all the more credence in the eyes of the community. Their response to a gurgle in the throat of a Pyncheon also reinforces it. Perhaps because they abhor the lowly but cannot openly scorn the gentry, the community has much to do with perpetuating a belief in the inheritance of the prophetic curse. Negative as such an inheritance may be, the people seem unable to resist the notion of inheritance; they thrive on whispering the original story amongst themselves and relish the authority of declaring that something like the gurgle in the throat must be connected to the curse.

The Pyncheon family is not the only one inheriting the traits of their ancestor. The characteristics of Matthew Maule are also said to live on in his descendants too. The Maules tend toward being reserved, which seems somehow connected with their mysterious powers over people's minds and dreams. But because it cannot be specifically delineated, this quality of reserve gains power. As the narrator describes Maule's descendants, "they had been marked out from other men—not strikingly, nor as with a sharp line, but with an effect that was felt, rather than spoken of—by an hereditary character of reserve" (26). This ambiguous quality prevents others from ever becoming too close to the Maules. Those who seek companionship with them "grew conscious of a circle roundabout the Maules, within the sanctity or the spell of which—in spite of an exterior of sufficient frankness and good-fellowship—it was impossible for any man to step" (26). There is something indefinite yet connected to the wizard-status given to their ancestor that the community offers as a reason for why none of them ever becomes close to a Maule.

And the community cites this quality of reserve as reason for why the Maules have remained among the lower classes. The poverty of the Maules, in turn, brings the influence of inheritance full circle in that "it certainly operated to prolong, in their case, and to confirm to them, as their only inheritance, those feelings of repugnance and superstitious terror with which the people of the town, even after awakening from their frenzy, continued to regard the memory of the reputed witches" (26). The story of the original curse gives the townspeople license to recoil from the unfortunate Maules. Yet the power of the idea of inheritance prevails: since no one can say for certain that inheritance does *not* justify the status and character of the Maules, it gains ground. On several levels, power is the subject here: the interior power of the Maules as opposed to the exterior power of the Pyncheons, and the powerful force of public and private perceptions of inheritance.

Thus, the family of Maule inherits the qualities of one who utters a curse. They become insignificant or oppressed in the worldly community, yet powerful in a mental or spiritual sense:

> The mantle, or rather, the ragged cloak of old Matthew Maule, had fallen upon his children. They were half-believed to inherit mysterious attributes; the family eye was said to possess strange power.

> Among other good-for-nothing properties and
> privileges, was one especially assigned them, of ex-
> ercising an influence over people's dreams. (26)

The descriptions of the influences of Maule's curse thus far
have been enough to indicate that they are far from "good-
for-nothing." Yet in so describing them, Hawthorne addresses the potential questions of skeptics, and thus enables
the reader to view the Maule capacity to influence dreams
with a less jaundiced eye. Also, in establishing that Maule's
descendants inherit the traits of their ancestor just as do
those of Colonel Pyncheon, the narrative establishes the
need for some sort of collaboration of their descendants in
order for restoration to take place.

As the narrative continues, we learn of further examples
of the persistence of the inheritance, such as the negative energy of Maule's Well in the garden and the dramatic physical
similarity of Judge Pyncheon to the original Colonel
Pyncheon. When Phoebe encounters the Judge, the narrator
speaks to the prophetic nature of the link between the two
Pyncheons, an observation that lies beyond Phoebe's mental
abilities. Like the temporally ambiguous quality of the prophetic perfect tense, this exchange shows prophecy as a union of past and present. Does the Judge's physical resemblance to the Colonel reflect, wonders Phoebe,

> a kind of prophecy? A deeper philosopher than
> Phoebe might have found something very terrible in
> this idea. It implied that the weaknesses and de-
> fects, the bad passions, the mean tendencies, and
> the moral diseases which lead to crime, are handed
> down from one generation to another, by a far surer
> process of transmission than human law has been

able to establish, in respect to the riches and honors which it seeks to entail upon posterity. (119)

Though innocent Phoebe senses something prophetic only on a surface level, the narrator indicates that a dark truth is implied herein. The similarities between the Colonel and the Judge point to the awful possibility that a tendency toward moral corruption and crime passes through the generations (a notion that haunted Hawthorne himself). While Phoebe does not consider the full implications of the inheritance, she nevertheless senses something negative that causes her to recoil from the Judge when he tries to kiss her.

As much as Phoebe actively dismisses, or fails to absorb, all things mysterious and superstitious, she is nevertheless impacted by the power of Maule's curse. At first, practical Phoebe had decided that the curse and subsequent inheritance was absurd.

> But ancient superstitions, after being steeped in human hearts and passing from lip to ear in manifold repetition, through a series of generations, become imbued with an effect of homely truth. The smoke of the domestic hearth has scented them, through and through. By long transmission among household facts, they grow to look like them, and have such a familiar way of making themselves at home, that their influence is usually greater than we suspect. (124)

This is the power of myth. These lines convey not only the pervasive effect of prophecy in *Seven Gables*, but also Hawthorne's project of giving mythic roots to American literature. Though the tales of Maule's curse begin as "ancient superstitions," they come to acquire a quality of truth that shapes the community, and perhaps even that community's sense of national identity.

The impact of stories from the early days of a nation with their quality of "homely truth," told over, and over again, gain a more powerful influence indeed. As opposed to the potential for transformation, restoration, or culmination that is often embodied in prophecy, superstition may grow, but it does not end. Neither is it connected, as is prophecy, with the individual's moral responsibility or action before the community or God. Upright, church-going Phoebe, determined as she is to dismiss all superstitious tales, nevertheless instinctually recoils at the gurgling sound in the Judge's throat. Therefore, there are two unsettling qualities of the power of the curse: first, that inclination to sin can be unavoidably inherited, and second that the notion of the inheritance itself has a far greater impact than logical reasoning grants it.

A determination that this influential and festering past should be wiped away appears in the person of Holgrave, who, as we come to learn at the end of the novel, is a descendent of Matthew Maule. Just as Ezekiel and other prophets revise the sour grapes proverb, Holgrave

> had that sense, or inward prophecy... that we are not doomed to creep on forever in the old bad way, but that, this very now, there are the harbingers abroad of a golden era, to be accomplished in his own lifetime. It seemed to Holgrave—as doubtless it has seemed to the hopeful of every century, since the epoch of Adam's grandchildren,—that in this age, more than ever before, the moss-grown and

185

rotten Past is to be torn down, and lifeless institu-
tions to be thrust out of the way, and their dead
corpses buried, and everything to begin anew. (179)

With Holgrave maintaining such a perspective, it comes as
no surprise when he plays an integral part in tearing down
the "rotten Past" to restore the relationship between the two
families. Here Hawthorne's use of "prophecy" implies a quality of knowing a timeless truth, rather than foreknowledge of
a future event. Once Holgrave and Phoebe fall in love, he
will adopt a more gradual perspective on restoration. Yet
here he calls for an immediate stop to the linear flow of time,
for a total dissolution of any connection whatsoever with the
past. This echoes Ezekiel's statement: "What mean ye, that
ye use this proverb concerning the land of Israel, saying, The
fathers have eaten sour grapes, and the children's teeth are
set on edge? As I live, saith the Lord GOD, ye shall not have
occasion any more to use this proverb in Israel" (18:2–3).
Likewise, Holgrave wants to put an end to the old proverb
that declares the failings of the previous generation to be
necessarily visited upon the subsequent generations.

Other characters would like to see an end to negative effects of the past as well. When he emerges from his passive
state, Clifford will voice a perspective like Holgrave's: that
permanent structures and old ways should be done away
with. While she yet struggles with relinquishing her status as
a lady, Hepzibah wishes for an end to the Pyncheon patterns
of greed as well. When Judge Pyncheon asks her to make
Clifford reveal the location of the alleged deed, Hepzibah
laments, "Alas, Cousin Jaffrey, this hard and grasping spirit
has run in our blood, these two hundred years! You are but
doing over again, in another shape, what your ancestor be-

186

fore you did, and sending down to your posterity the curse inherited from him!" (237). Hepzibah fully acknowledges her own part in the inheritance; she has the self-knowledge other Pyncheons lack, admitting that a "hard and grasping spirit has run in [their] blood." This fits with the "to desire" or "to try to get" meaning of the name Hepzibah. The various implications of the name in the two places in the Hebrew Bible, "to try to get" or "to delight in" fit the positive transformative experiences Hepzibah undergoes in the novel. In her words to her cousin, Hepzibah speaks of the curse as something that is both inherited and that the individual is responsible for perpetuating. The implications are that she and the Judge do inherit a tendency toward greed, but they have the responsibility to resist that tendency.[9] The cruel Judge determines this notion of inheritance to be nonsense, yet in placing the "voice of reason" in one as heartless and insensitive as the Judge, Hawthorne further validates the notion that resisting the inheritance of the curse is a necessary struggle.

If this is the case, what are we to make of the moment in the text when Holgrave would seem to undercut the curse?

---

[9] Gracia Fay Ellwood rightly observes that, "Hepzibah isn't greedy in the active sense of the Colonel and the Judge—in fact she was willing to die of hunger when her money ran out. It was love for Clifford that wouldn't let her do so. But she did want to cling to the past in hanging on to her status as a Lady, i.e., one who lived off others' labor. She was willing to deny herself, however, and work to support Clifford. Thus, her active love, despite the pain it causes her, can be said to cancel out the curse in the sense that she is foregoing her Pyncheon inheritance" (10 January 2010).

When he and Phoebe meet in the house, empty but for the dead body of Judge Pyncheon, Holgrave speaks of a physical condition in the Pyncheon family as the cause of death:

> This mode of death has been an idiosyncrasy with his family, for generations past; not often occurring, indeed, but—when it does occur—usually attacking individuals of about the Judge's time of life, and generally in the tension of some mental crisis, or perhaps in an access of wrath. Old Maule's prophecy was probably founded on a knowledge of this physical predisposition in the Pyncheon race. (304)

Is the power of Maule's curse over the Pyncheons undone by this simple fact of a medical condition? Surely the shaping themes of the novel, the prophetic curse and sinful inheritance, are not to be undercut by one statement, unsupported by any other source, document, or character. In a typical Hawthornian move, we are given a purely rational but thoroughly unconvincing explanation. Still, this information is offered by Holgrave, a character who is honest and kind in his transactions with the other characters. He proves himself trustworthy through resisting the temptation to control Phoebe's mind. And yet, in that particular, the notion of inheritance is again validated: Holgrave is presented as having the Maule predisposition to control people's dreams, to have the capacity for mesmerism that ruined poor Alice Pyncheon's life. Holgrave's story does enchant Phoebe, yet he does not take advantage of her vulnerable mental state. It could it be that he does not do so because there really was no such thing as an inherited characteristic of mesmerism in the first place. While this is a possibility, Hawthorne does not lure us toward adapting this perspective. Neither does the above passage regarding a Pyncheon medical condition convince the average reader to dismiss a belief in the power of Maule's curse. From this "explanation" we emerge further convinced of the power of inheritance.

For in his way, Holgrave also believes in the curse. In view of the evidence that misery and death has come upon the people who have lived in the house, Holgrave has no doubt that Colonel Pyncheon's unnatural attempt to "plant a family" has led to generations of misfortune. When Phoebe tells Holgrave that such a sensible man as he should not believe in superstitions, Holgrave responds,

> "I do believe it," said the artist seriously—"not as a superstition, however—but as proved by unquestionable facts, and as exemplifying a theory. Now, see! Under those seven gables, at which we now look up—...under that roof, through a portion of three centuries, there has been perpetual remorse of conscience, a constantly defeated hope, strife amongst kindred, various misery, a strange form of death, dark suspicion, unspeakable disgrace,—all, or most of which calamity, I have the means of tracing to the old Puritan's inordinate desire to plant and endow a family. To plant a family! This idea is at the bottom of most of the wrong and mischief which men do. The truth is, that, once in every half-century, at longest, a family should be merged into the great, obscure mass of humanity, and forget all about its ancestors." (185)

Holgrave's fact-based philosophy views the Colonel's great wrong, indeed the great wrong of most men, as his "inordinate desire to plant and endow a family." Prefiguring Thomas Sutpen's doomed mission to start a dynasty in Faulkner's *Absalom, Absalom!*, the Colonel's violation of the land and the life of another in order to establish his own dynasty leads to his and his family's misery. For Holgrave, it is not Maule's curse, but the fact of Maule's oppression and murder that leads to the generational inheritance of misfortune in the Pyncheon line.

And how is this inheritance to be undone? Neither a medical explanation nor an account of a theory will bring about change. It is undone through encounters with the prophetic perfect, through compassionate hearts entering new relationship with time. Holgrave offers his own version of this. According to his theory, the opportunity will come if "once in every half-century, at longest, a family should be merged into the great, obscure mass of humanity, and forget all about its ancestors" (185). Holgrave calls for a total break from the past, for ancestors to be forgotten and for people to experience anonymity. As he explains passionately to Phoebe, the weight of the past should be obliterated:

> Whatever we seek to do, of our own free motion, a Dead Man's icy hand obstructs us! Turn our eyes to what point we may, a Dead Man's white, immitigable face encounters them, and freezes our very heart! And we must be dead ourselves, before we can begin to have our proper influence on our own world, which will then be no longer our world, but the world of another generation, with which we shall have no shadow of a right to interfere. I ought to have said, too, that we live in Dead Men's houses; as, for instance, in this of the seven gables! (183)

Holgrave goes on to declare that the seven-gabled house should be burned to the ground, should be purified with fire.[10] His radical stance is that the only way to emerge from the negative influence of the past is to detach the present from it utterly and completely. We must be skeptical of Holgrave's extreme call to burn old structures to the ground, completely disassociate with one's ancestors, and utterly remove the heavy hand of the Dead Man so that this world will belong to the present. Living entirely for the future is no more productive (or realistic) than is dwelling entirely in the past. Of course, biblical prophetic visions of restoration may sometimes be hyperbolic or idealistic visions of complete transformation of a present situation. Yet when Holgrave falls in love and restoration takes place, he will come to advocate the kind of harmonious unity of past, present, and future that Uncle Venner embodies throughout the novel.

Besides their biblical parallel with purification through fire, Holgrave's sentiments echo those of renewal found in Revelation. The removal of despair and of death are part of this vision of a new heaven and a new earth: "And God shall wipe away all tears from their eyes; and there shall be no more death, neither sorrow, nor crying, neither shall there be any more pain: for the former things are passed away" (Revelation 21:4). This well-known New Testament passage is of course a prophetic promise. And in his way, Holgrave is a prophet figure. He holds forth regarding his vision of absolute restoration, and passionately articulates the way in which

---

[10] Purification through fire, or allusion to such, appears in numerous texts—including prophetic texts—in the Hebrew Bible. It is based on priestly purification ritual traditions.

he understands it to be possible. But the moment of love and timelessness he experiences with Phoebe will temper his vision so that it centers around a hopeful future will not to be based exclusively on it.

Clifford proves to be a prophet as well, likewise advocating for the destruction of old structures and a break from the past. But he also maintains a sensitivity to the beauty and importance of transformative growth. When Clifford emerges from his stupor and takes Hepzibah with him on the train, he detaches himself from the spell of the house and suddenly become the voice of change. Until this point, Hepzibah was the abler of the pair. She looked after Clifford and took steps to separate herself from the past through her brave efforts in opening the cent shop. She knows that change must come, and she can sense its imminence as the novel progresses. When the Judge comes to force Clifford to reveal the deed, Hepzibah "could not rid herself of the sense of something unprecedented, at that instant passing, and soon to be accomplished" (241). Hepzibah's sensitivity enables her to perceive that something must give, but does not necessarily provide the energy or presence of mind to bring change to full fruition. Her desire for transition, especially at this moment in the novel, for "anything that would take her out of the grievous present," is ultimately satisfied through Clifford's actions (242).[11] This is not wholly unlike Holgrave's prophecy of change; stasis is deadly. When Clifford takes them onto

---

[11] Another example of Hepzibah initiating a change that is more fully realized through the work of another, is in the cent shop. She musters all her emotional strength to open it, but it is Phoebe's cheerful energy that turns in to an actual success.

the train and it begins to move, he has enabled a break from the house that his sister's spirit needed, but only he was finally able to carry out.

As the train pulls away from the station and the dark, wet landscape begins to flash past, Clifford enters a new dimension, one that perhaps echoes Catharine's trance state in "The Gentle Boy." In the midst of the crowd on the moving train they live out Holgrave's prophetic call for families to merge into the obscurity of humanity: "At last, therefore, and after so long estrangement from everything that the world acted or enjoyed, they had been drawn into the great current of human life, and were swept away with it, as by the suction of fate itself" (256). They had lived under the weight of the past and its dead for so long that Hepzibah wonders if this strange immersion could be a dream. But Clifford responds, "'A dream, Hepzibah!' repeated he, almost laughing in her face. 'On the contrary, I have never been awake before!'" (256). Hepzibah worries that Clifford is going mad, and that perhaps she herself is not far from it: "Happy! He is mad already; and, if I could once feel myself broad awake, I should go mad too!" (258). But Clifford is indeed awakened to a new reality, and he becomes a prophet proclaiming the virtues of that new reality. Prophets are often viewed as treading the threshold between madness and lucidity, and Hepzibah and the old gentleman on the train grow uncomfortable with his bold declarations. But Clifford is finally at peace through a realization of Holgrave's vision: he has let go of the past, is disconnected from the burden of time, and is caught up in the motion of life.

The release from the weight of the house and the movement of the train prompt Clifford to utter his own vision on the progressively cyclical nature of life and the human tendency to return to a nomadic way of being. The old gentleman speaks of the comforts of hearth and home, but Clifford sees the nomadic state as ideal, and declares that,

> all human progress is…in an ascending spiral curve. While we fancy ourselves going straight forward, and attaining, at every step, an entirely new position of affairs, we do actually return to something long ago tried and abandoned, but which we now find etherealized, refined, and perfected to its ideal. The past is but a coarse and sensual prophecy of the present and the future. (259–260)

Clifford's optimistic vision involves not a total break from the past, but a new understanding of the relationship among past, present, and future: a return to an original idea that is refined into an ideal.[12] Clifford's delight in the moment enables him to envision a hope for humanity that is not unlike Ezekiel's vision of the restored temple, which is far grander (and the people's relationship with God more pure) than was the original temple and the worship that once took place there. The ideal is not utterly changed from tradition: there will still be a temple, and the old, but now purified, rituals will again take place. Likewise for Clifford, there is a forward flow to time, but progressing upward from the past is crucial for his achieving this vision. As Carey McWilliams has ob-

---

[12] Julian C. Rice posits that "Of all the passengers, however, Clifford is the only one fully aware of and delighting in the moment. Movement, Hawthorne suggests, exists only for those who, like Holgrave, and now Clifford, are awake to it" (57).

served "The railroad was Pyncheon's ideal, his hope for end-less motion; the electric telegraph would spiritualize matter, making the whole country—or even the world—a nerve throbbing with love" (McWilliams 316).

The further the train moves away from the house, the more youthful Clifford's physical features and energy be-come, and the more elated his demeanor. Clifford works himself up to an excited state, but, like a prophet emerging from a trance, he falls virtually silent as soon as they leave the train and step out onto the lonely station platform: "A pow-erful excitement had given him energy and vivacity. Its oper-ation over, he forthwith began to sink. 'You must take the lead now, Hepzibah!' murmured he, with a torpid and reluc-tant utterance. 'Do with me as you will!'" (266). Hepzibah's response is to kneel and pray to God for mercy. Perhaps that prayer is answered, for the next time we see the brother and sister, they have safely but mysteriously returned to the house. Clifford's prophetic revelation, his call for renewal, closely resembles Holgrave's: both begin to lose their radical vision once they return to a traditional relationship to time and space. But the moments of transcendence they experi-ence propel them, and the people who love them, toward positive change.

Not all critics view Clifford's ecstatic overtures on the train as viable prophetic utterances. In his book, *Mesmerism and Hawthorne*, Samuel Chase Coale proposes that the old gentleman's distaste for Clifford's revelations indicates their ridiculous, ineffectual nature: "lest we fall for such nonsense, Hawthorne is careful to fill the gentleman to whom Clifford is speaking with doubts and describes him as having a 'gimlet eye…determined to bore right into him'" (94). This analysis lacks sensitivity to Hawthorne's careful diction. The gentleman is justifiably uncomfortable with Clifford's declarations, but the description of his "gimlet eye...determined to bore right into him" casts a negative energy over this man. It renders him the unenlightened one who stands in contrast with the lighthearted, exuberant Clifford who is given a voice to speak after years of silent despair. Granted, Hawthorne's prophet figures who enter trance states, such as Catharine in "The Gentle Boy," are flawed characters, but there is nevertheless truth in what they say. And in this instance, the personal growth that Clifford's revelation indicates is purely positive. Coale proceeds to argue that Hepzibah is right to call him mad, and that she seeks God's mercy on the platform in despair over Clifford's wild behavior: "so much for prophetic visions and actual circumstances" Coale concludes (94). But it is through Clifford's prophetic visions that he becomes able to move forward from his past. Hepzibah's prayer is her sincerest effort to seek help now that Clifford has relinquished his temporary authority. It reflects her fear of what will become of the two of them now that they stand alone in a deserted train station, and her faith that a merciful God will guide them to safety.

As Hepzibah's answered prayer suggests, human beings are not the sole agents effecting change. In biblical texts, prophets are vehicles through whom God works. Hawthorne rarely, if ever, imbues his novels with an overtly Christian message. But John Gatta reminds us that the concept of

Providence[13] is nevertheless taken quite seriously in Hawthorne's works:

> a belief in Providence, in the ever mysterious but ultimately benevolent designs of a hidden God, was one of the few points of Christian theology to which Hawthorne himself gave fairly explicit creedal assent. ...The idea of Providence can explain a good deal about the structure and ordering of his narrative and stands in this book as the final measure against which all progress must be judged. (Gatta, "Progress and Providence in *The House of the Seven Gables*," 39)

Citing Hawthorne's fondness of Bunyan's *The Pilgrim's Progress*, Gatta suggests that "Hawthorne's romance affirms the reality—indeed, the necessity—of the individual pilgrim's progress" (42). Of Hawthorne's novels, *Seven Gables* comes the closest to representing a world guided by a compassionate God who serves as the ultimate source of positive change.

---

[13] F. O. Matthiessen also sees the prevalence of Providence in that the nineteenth-century "tendency of American idealism to see a spiritual significance in every natural fact was far more broadly diffused than transcendentalism. Loosely Platonic, it came specifically from the common background that lay behind Emerson and Hawthorne, from the Christian habit of mind that saw the hand of God in all manifestations of life, and which, in the intensity of the New England seventeenth century, had gone to the extreme of finding 'remarkable providences' even in the smallest phenomena, tokens of divine displeasure in every capsized dory or runaway cow" (Matthiessen 243).

Francis Battaglia also affirms the presence of a benevolent divine agent at work in the novel:

> The agency behind the transformations is the mercy of God. Hawthorne playfully allows the inference that God is the agent when he says the House 'really' looked as if it had a happy history. For that description seems feasible only in light of his earlier statement that "God is the sole worker of realities." (Battaglia, *The House of the Seven Gables*: New Light on Old Problems," 587)

Battaglia explores these and other examples of the centrality of God throughout the novel. He supports this with evidence such as Hawthorne's description of the light falling into the house after Judge Pyncheon's death as a "universal benediction, annulling evil, and rendering all goodness possible, and happiness attainable....This new day...God has smiled upon, and blessed, and given to mankind" (588). Battaglia reads this as an actual, rather than an ironic, discussion of God's involvement in the restoration. He states that, "The Mercy of God can always be explained as inexplicable, but Hawthorne has given us a better account of its workings within his story" (588). God is also at work through Hepzibah's struggling faith that culminates in her prayer on the train platform. Her and Clifford's safe arrival back at the house and the ending that is nothing if not merciful indicates that her prayer for mercy was realized (588).

If God is working through the biblically named Hepzibah, it is not surprising that she too makes prophetic utterances, which Battaglia's analysis also brings to the fore. Before the train excursion, Hepzibah's insistence on a merciful God is already evident, and her warnings to Judge Pyncheon prove to be justified: "God will not let you do the thing you meditate!" Hepzibah declares in response to the Judge's forcing Clifford for the deed (237). And lo, death prevents the Judge from pressing Clifford for the (now expired) deed. Battaglia states that in insisting on speaking to Clifford, "Judge Pyncheon, the man of affairs, had ignored his old maid cousin's unwittingly prophetical warning" (589). Yet is Hepzibah's prophecy completely unwitting? While she does not overflow with a confidence in the truth of her own claim, she nevertheless does appear sincerely to believe—or sincerely to strive toward believing—in a God who would not let such a man as the Judge oppress such a man as her brother Clifford. Even when the Judge insists, when there is no longer any avenue for retreat, a cry for mercy issues forth from Hepzibah that foreshadows her prayer at the train station: "Be merciful in your dealings with him!—be far more merciful than your heart bids you be!—for God is looking at you Jaffrey Pyncheon!" (238). As Battaglia suggests, "at this point it is evident that Hepzibah believes a watchful heaven is mindful of Clifford's plight" (588). Regardless of her awareness of her prophetic abilities, Hepzibah, in her compassion for her brother, serves here as a mouthpiece of God, rightly foretelling that the Judge will be prevented from torturing Clifford, and insisting on the mercy of God.

Throughout the novel, Hepzibah has striven to swallow her aristocratic pride to provide for her brother. She now calls on Judge Pyncheon likewise to let go of the Pyncheon sense of entitlement and to have mercy on Clifford. Julian C. Rice connects the letting go of pride with making space for compassion:

The insignificance of individual existence and striving, when finally recognized by ambitious people, liberates them and brings about the consummation of love. It is pride that kills and petrifies, not physical death, which is only a part of nature. Petrification, as personified by Hepzibah and Clifford, is also isolation. (54)

The novel bears witness to both Hepzibah and Clifford in various states of petrification before they each grow more flexible through their compassion and an openness to redefining their relationship to time. The heartless Judge, of course, will refuse to do this, and in death he will sit petrified in the family chair as the ancestral shadows obliterate him in darkness.

The Judge will not accept his own insignificance and as such he is incapable of mercy. In contrast, Holgrave is the greatest champion of accepting the insignificance of the individual. His concern with the loss of the self accords with Rice's remark that, "Change, on the other hand, must be celebrated and accepted, even if it reminds us of life's transience and the relative insignificance of the individual" (54). While Holgrave held forth earlier regarding his theory on the need for the destruction of the rotten past, the transformative moment from which he emerges truly changes his encounter with Phoebe in the vacated house. A timeless sacredness envelops the space as Phoebe and Holgrave share their love with one another:

And it was in this hour, so full of doubt and awe, that the one miracle was wrought, without which every human existence is a blank. The bliss, which makes all things true, beautiful, and holy, shone around this youth and maiden. They were conscious of nothing sad nor old. They transfigured the earth, and made it Eden again, and themselves the two first dwellers in it. The dead man, so close beside them, was forgotten. At such a crisis, there is no Death; for Immortality is revealed anew, and embraces everything in its hallowed atmosphere. (307)

This moment of bliss is characterized by complete unawareness of anything old. Holgrave's vision of restoration is realized, not as he once described it—as a physical tearing down of old structures and lineages—but, more like Clifford's vision, of a spiritual or emotional transcendence of death through love.[14]

The love of Holgrave and Phoebe is selfless; perhaps it could be described as mutual mercifulness. As such, and in uniting the two families of Maule and Pyncheon, it brings an end to the Pyncheon heritage of greed. The language of sacred space and timelessness surrounds the young couple as they stand in the house, having lost track of everything around them except each other marks the undoing of the curse. Gatta explores the power of this union, writing that that

the central sign of an apocalyptic climax, especially when we recall the cosmic marriage celebrated in the Book of Revelaiton, is the alliance between Holgrave and Phoebe as discussed in almost vision-

---

[14] "The claim to aristocracy has come to an end in Clifford's degradation, Hepzibah's sacrificial renunciation of the status of Lady, and Phoebe's being the innocent she always was" (Gracia Fay Ellwood 10 February 2010).

ary terms. For one enchanted moment, anyway, the
couple is supposedly able to throw off the dead
weight of time, which has dominated the Judge's
"vigil" in Chapter 18, and enter a realized state of
eschatology in which "immortality is revealed anew,
and embraces everything." (Gatta, 47)

Time dissolves for Phoebe and Holgrave in chapter twenty,
"The Flower of Eden." In contrast, time is at its most oppressive surrounding the depiction of the dead judge in chapter eighteen, "Governor Pyncheon." This transitional chapter, heavy with repeated mentions of time, labors under the
suffocating fulfillment of the curse.

In, "Governor Pyncheon," the Judge sits dead and the
house's shadows grow and deepen around him. The theme of
time, repeated throughout the chapter in the missed ap-
pointments of the Judge, and the eerie ticking of the dead
man's watch, prefigures "Time Passes" in Woolf's *To the
Lighthouse*.[15] No one lives in the dwelling that once held so
much life, and such despair. Yet still shadows gather in the
rooms and wind blows about the empty structure, while the
Judge is dead in his chair.

> Meanwhile the twilight is glooming upward out of
> the corners of the room. The shadows of the tall
> furniture grow deeper, and at first become more
> definite; then, spreading wider, they lose their dis-
> tinctness of outline in the dark, gray tide of oblivi-

---

[15] For a discussion on the similarities between these two
works, see John B. Humma, "'Time Passes' in *To the Lighthouse*;
'Governor Pyncheon' in *The House of the Seven Gables*."

on, as it were, that creeps slowly over the various objects, and the one human figure sitting in the midst of them...And how looks it now? There is no window! There is no face! An infinite, inscrutable blackness has annihilated sight! Where is our universe? All crumbled away from us; and we, adrift in chaos, may hearken to the gusts of homeless wind, that go sighing and murmuring about, in quest of what was once a world! (276)

Throughout this section, Hawthorne explores time in relationship to a dead man. Holgrave earlier spoke of a Dead Man as oppressing the house and all who dwell therein. No longer do the dead oppress this house; now the house itself overwhelms the dead man. As Judge Pyncheon misses meetings and luncheons, the house's shadows gradually obscure him into total darkness and an insignificance that eerily echoes Holgrave's call for humanity to transcend the weight of the past. The curse is again fulfilled, and the Judge, who once had Clifford cowering before him, now sits erased in blackness while Clifford grows ever more alive on the train that's gliding through the night. In this passage, Hawthorne narrates a visual movement toward obscurity. In unsettling contrast with the positive features of timelessness elsewhere in the novel, here timelessness is associated with death; the shadows first grow sharper, and then their edges begin to soften by degrees. Unlike other transformative instances in which characters break from the past by stepping outside of time, here we find an exclusive focus on time as a force for erasing that which was once a source of oppressive power: Judge Pyncheon.

With the Judge dead and the two families of Maule and Pyncheon united in the relationship between Phoebe and Holgrave, the heaviness of the past inheritance lifts for the four protagonists who depart for the country. Yet, the narrator stays with the two "characters" who will never cease to exist apart from their association with the past: the house itself, and Maule's well. Earlier in the novel, the well is described as having a degree of prophetic, or otherwise unnatural power. Holgrave somewhat jokingly tells Phoebe not to drink from nor wash her face with its water because "it is water bewitched!" (94). When Clifford takes his afternoons in the garden, he stands over the well watching a shifting parade of faces gaze up at him. The narrator tells us that the lovely faces reflect his character, and the awful ones announce his fate (153–154). Then in the final paragraph the narrator again rests on the well, which, with no one to gaze into it, still offers prophetic images:

> Maule's well, all this time, though left in solitude, was throwing up a succession of kaleidoscopic pictures, in which a gifted eye might have seen foreshadowed the coming fortunes of Hepzibah, and Clifford, and the descendant of the legendary wizard, and the village-maiden, over whom he had thrown love's web of sorcery. The Pyncheon-elm moreover, with what foliage the September gale had spared to it, whispered unintelligible prophecies. And wise Uncle Venner, passing slowly from the ruinous porch, seemed to hear a strain of music, and fancied that sweet Alice Pyncheon—after witnessing these deeds, this by-gone woe, and this present happiness, of her kindred mortals—had given one

farewell touch of a spirit's joy upon her harpsichord, as she floated heavenward from the HOUSE OF THE SEVEN GABLES! (319)

The theme of prophecy appears in this novel's closing lines, just as it does in those of *The Scarlet Letter*. Here the final paragraph speaks of the protagonists as characters in a legend. One capable of prophetic divination might have seen Clifford's and Hepzibah's fate already prophesied by the well. Holgrave becomes "the descendent of the legendary wizard" who casts a spell over Phoebe. For all his gestures toward reason and empirical evidence and his merit gained for resisting the temptation to mesmerize Phoebe, here is Holgrave as a sorcerer. Though the characters themselves seem to have overcome the burden of the inheritance of the past, there is no escaping the vocabulary charged with sorcery and prophecy that supports this narrative.

As the story draws to a close, the elm tree that casts shade over the scene "whispered unintelligible prophecies." The concept of prophecy, here as in *The Scarlet Letter*, has a future-telling quality that nature comprehends and speaks of, but in a language that humanity cannot understand. The Pyncheon-elm echoes the brook in *The Scarlet Letter*'s "A Forest Walk" that "would not be comforted, and still kept telling its unintelligible secret of some very mournful mystery that had happened—or making a prophetic lamentation about something that was yet to happen" (187). In *Seven Gables*, the tree, the house, the well, will forever have the power to lament and to prophesy, while the people work toward overcoming their negative associations with the past.

But there is one who lives in healthy relationship with the past, present, and future throughout the course of the novel: Uncle Venner. That he lives apart from the house and its burden of course plays a role in his lighthearted worldview. Nevertheless, he is sensitive to the past, dwells thoughtfully in the present, and maintains a hopeful outlook on the future. This contrasts with Clifford and Holgrave, for example, who are not capable, at least initially, of living in harmonious association with the past. They call for a full restoration of the past, while Uncle Venner, who has not lived under the weight of the Pyncheon estate, lives in comfortable relationship with it. In some ways he resembles Dickens' Ghost of Christmas Past who embodies both youth and old age. And here in the closing image and sounds of the story, "wise Uncle Venner" fancies he hears the spirit of Alice Pyncheon playing a chord of joy on her harpsichord before her ghost lifts out of the house and up to heaven. We suspect this is more than a fantasy—that Alice's ghost metaphorically was trapped under the weight of the family conflict and has finally been released of her earthly attachment to the House of the Seven Gables. Her happy liberation comes after the restoration of the family relationships through the combined actions of the four protagonists. Moreover, her fleeting appearance in the narrative's closing sentence lends substance to all the ghostly, shadowy, prophetic elements of the story. The living characters' moments of temporal transcendence paired with their loving concern for one another enable them to revise the proverb of generational inheritance, which in turn frees Alice from her earthly entrapment by the house. Clifford's vision of restoration as purified migration is realized in his and his companions' removal to the country, but his prophecy also comes to pass in Alice's upward migration toward heaven.

Timelessness—a reflection of the prophetic perfect—
must be achieved in some way by each of the protagonists for
the curse to be lifted. Phoebe never allows the weight of the
house to crush her; instead, she gives life and light, as her
name suggests, to the other three. The moment of love, of
timelessness, that she shares with Holgrave brings about full
closure to the prophecy. Holgrave's participation in that sacred moment is of course needed to end the curse. His radical but sincere prophecies about a dissociation from the past
through an anonymous immersion in the currents of humanity plays a necessary role in restoration, and Clifford's embodiment of them enables his own prophetic vision.
Hepzibah strives toward the prophetic perfect—or at least
out of stasis and into transformation—when she breaks from
her aristocratic heritage out of love for her brother and
achieves it through expressing faith in a merciful God despite a lifetime of disappointments and injustices. And
Clifford's prophetic declarations on the speeding train not
only represent his own liberation; his vision of an ascending
spiral foreshadows the final image of a full restoration for
one who had been suffering through the generations: Alice
Pyncheon's ghost.

In his essay on Providence and *Seven Gables*, John Gatta
speaks, in so many words, of this prophetic perfect:

> Hawthorne's book insists that the Kingdom cannot
> be brought visibly to birth in society through delib-
> erate human exertion. Instead its progressive emer-
> gence in the world is secret, invisible, coexistent
> with the seemingly more substantial stuff of fallen
> human history. For Hawthorne the eternal essence
> of the spiritual Kingdom is paradoxically here al-

ready and not here yet—but it is never to be glimpsed through the unworthy eyes of a Jaffrey Pyncheon. (Gatta, 46)

Gatta uses language of the Kingdom to describe that which is eternally present, but also still to come. Yet "human exertion" can and does play a role in bringing about restoration in *Seven Gables*. True, the protagonists must enter new relationships with temporality to open doors to the unknown and the sacred. But they do not stumble blindly upon these moments: their compassion-based efforts to move forward put them on the path toward prophetic perfect realities. Though Hepzibah's merciful God answers prayers, the hope for restoration lies in the able hands of an upwardly migrating humanity.

In *The House of the Seven Gables*, as in many of Hawthorne's prophet stories, people must act to evince change. Movement is imperative for the characters to break free from Maule's prophecy and their perceived static identities. George Shulman turns to Thoreau to highlight prophecy's power of forward momentum:

Prophecy can elevate people's 'expectations and requirements,' Thoreau says, by animating values they imagine as static, dramatizing commitments they reify by forgetting, and energizing democratic solidarities they invoke in name only. In these and other ways, prophetic visions, questions, claims, demands, and energy—provoking, recalcitrant, haunting, passionate, and poetic—may be especially needful now" (Shulman, xvi).

These aspects of prophecy have been and will ever be needful—in every generation. Nostalgic as we may be for our idealized concepts of our national origins, *Seven Gables* reminds us that movement is imperative, that generations must shift for humanity to step out of stasis and into growth. With this text, Hawthorne moves backward and forward at the same time: an old curse and a gloomy mansion laden with shadows and secrets is captivating. We will step into those shadows; they intrigue us. We may be lulled into thinking they define us. But we cannot stay there. Prophetic imagination—at once ancient and futuristic—calls us to hear and use the voices of the past to create our present and future agency.

Conclusion

Blithedale and Beyond

And what of *The Blithedale Romance*? I have not explored prophecy in *Blithedale* because my focus is on Hawthorne's Puritan based narratives and their identity as literary origin myths for America. But, unsurprisingly, prophecy informs this roughly contemporary novel, too. The very first sentence of *Blithedale* is about the mysterious "Veiled Lady." Before we hear from her, however, we are subjected to the narrator's dubious views on the fad of mesmerism and the reality that a present-day "exhibitor" is sensible enough to present the work of his "'subject,' 'clairvoyant,' or 'medium,'" as a sort of scientific experiment. And though this novel is set in the nineteenth century, Hawthorne still manages to push it slightly into the past—roughly fifteen years before the "present day" of our first-person narrator, Coverdale. And that is enough to evolve a shift in community perceptions of prophetic language. For just a short fifteen years earlier, "all the arts of mysterious arrangement, of picturesque disposition, and artistically contrasted light and shade, were made available in order to set the apparent miracle in the strongest attitude of opposition to ordinary facts" (6). Clearly this is all a show, and the dim view the narrator takes of such exhibitions strays not far from Hawthorne's own view of nine-teenth century mesmerism mania.[1]

And if the exhibitor is a charlatan, then the medium herself is presented as victim, not scam-artist. The Veiled Lady is not only a sad figure; she is an ineffectual one. In the first chapter of *Blithedale*, Coverdale asks her to prophesy about whether the Blithedale Farm experiment will be suc-cessful. The Veiled Lady—as we will come to understand—is Priscilla, and her "prophecy" matches the sort of vague, one-size-fits-all quality of many a generic omen: "The re-sponse, by-the-by, was of the true Sibylline stamp, nonsensi-cal in its first aspect, yet, on closer study, unfolding a variety of interpretations, one of which has certainly accorded with the event. I was turning over this riddle in my mind, and try-ing to catch its slippery purport by the tail, when the old man, above-mentioned, interrupted me" (6). This bodes well neither for the Veiled Lady's prophetic abilities nor the Blithedale Farm's prospects. If the Veiled Lady is a prophet, it is only in show.

---

[1] In an 1841 letter to his wife Sophia, Hawthorne writes at length against the practice of mesmerism and his deep concern that she not participate in it: "But, belovedest, my spirit is moved to talk to thee to day about these magnetic miracles, and to be-seech thee to take no part in them. I am unwilling that a power should be exercised on thee, of which we know neither the origin nor the consequence, and the phenomena of which seem rather calculated to bewilder us, than to teach us any truths about the present or future state of being" (Hawthorne, *The Blithedale Ro-mance*: Norton Critical Edition, 242).

Even the town rumors about Priscilla when she was young—that she had a "gift of second-sight and prophecy"—are based on the townspeople's perceptions of her, not demonstrable prophetic actions. After explaining that Priscilla's longings for an absent mother and sister prompt her sad, silent nature, the narrator tells us that the townsfolk have come to their own conclusions about her pale, retreating nature:

> The gross and simple neighbors whispered strange things about Priscilla. The big, red, Irish matrons, whose innumerable progeny swarmed out of the adjacent doors, used to mock at the pale Western child. They fancied—or, at least, affirmed it, between jest and earnest—that she was not so solid flesh and blood as other children, but mixed largely with a thinner element. They called her ghost-child, and said that she could indeed vanish, when she pleased, but could never, in her densest moments, make herself quite visible... Hidden things were visible to her, (at least, so the people inferred from obscure hints, escaping unawares out of her mouth,) and silence was audible. And, in all the world, there was nothing so difficult to be endured, by those who had any dark secret to conceal, as the glance of Priscilla's timid and melancholy eyes. (187)

Tales of Priscilla's sub- or super-human status stem from community gossip. We see in these lines echoes of the big Puritan women shaming Hester on the scaffold, or the way in which Reverend Hooper's veil compels onlookers to feel as though he knows what is in their hearts. Here, as in *The Scarlet Letter* and "The Minister's Black Veil," Hawthorne gives us a sad but sympathetic prophet figure whose isolation is magnified by the judgments of the townsfolk.

There is a sadness inherent in all of Hawthorne's prophet figures. Priscilla's captivity is eased only by the temporary hope of the doomed Blithedale Farm. And that short-lived experiment reflects Hawthorne's disillusionment with American Transcendentalism, a disillusionment that aligns not with despair over what's possible for America, but in his discomfort with American Exceptionalism. In *The Blithedale Romance*, as in Hawthorne's other national identity stories, the idea of a single, unified vision upon which we all must lean to "be Americans" dissolves—mercifully—into Hawthornian ambiguity and the prophets who dwell in that liminal space.

Hawthorne's fiction teems with such prophets. They bring about transformation, utter prophecies of doom and restoration, liberate individuals, and open the hearts of entire communities. Moreover, Hawthorne makes worlds that need prophets in order to grow. He also creates niches from which prophets emerge. They align with Walter Brueggemann's concept of the spheres out of which prophets are born:

> —the subcommunity that may generate prophecy will participate in the public life of the dominant community; it does so, however, from a certain perspective and with a certain intention. Such a subcommunity is likely to be one in which

> —there is a *long and available memory* that sinks the present generation deep into an identifiable past that is available in song and story;

214

—there is an available, expressed sense of pain that is owned and recited as a real social fact, that is visibly acknowledged in a public way, and that is understood as unbearable for the long term;

—there is an active practice of hope, a community that knows about promises yet to be kept, promises that stand in judgment on the present. (*The Prophetic Imagination*, xvi)

In their capacity to understand pain, Hawthorne's prophets rely on the memory of that pain to bring about restoration. They must also "participate in the public life of the dominant community" as those who share in the community's pain and its perversions. Through this participation they are also able to address the state of the community, and or their own conditions. A memory of a time of unity or harmony is necessary too; the prophet who remembers humanity's potential for goodness can draw from that memory in her work. Affirming memories can also enable the prophet when a seemingly hopeless situation may stunt her once compassionate nature. It is the prophet's compassion that finally enables her to bring her own song into concert with that of the community.

The relationship between prophet and community is necessarily challenging. It involves a declaration that people have been making mistakes, or perhaps a refusal to accept or participate in sinful actions no matter how deeply they are imbedded in the memory or culture of the community. As Heschel asserts, that stance involves saying *No* to an accepted but problematic norm. But it begins with a capacity to disassociate oneself from a numbing status quo and to engage in lamentation: "real criticism begins in the capacity to grieve because that is the most visceral announcement that things are not right" (Brueggemann 11). Though we are not privy to the thoughts of the Gray Champion, some understanding or experience of grief spurs the prophetic works of Catharine, Hooper, Hester, Hepzibah, Clifford, and Holgrave. And it is the loss of an ability to grieve that forces Richard Digby out of the status of prophet.

Being awake to grief requires a connection with the past. If Tamar of 2 Samuel 13 had simply accepted her new status as a violated woman whose brokenness reflected the crumbling Davidic line, she would not have put ashes on her head, torn her royal gown, and cried out in despair over the loss of her virginity and her family's righteousness. That would require a process of numbing that results in passive acceptance. But Tamar, full of wisdom and compassion, grieves. She has the capacity to become a powerful prophet. But it is difficult to live and act out of compassion after an experience of grief. It involves retaining links with a painful past while opening eyes toward the future in the midst of a desperate or hopeless situation.

Brueggemann describes the hopelessness of the "royal consciousness," the mentality behind the kingdoms of Pharaoh in the Exodus narratives and Solomon in the Kings narratives. Prophets cry out against royal regimes because they portend

> to be the full and final ordering. That claim means that there can be no future that either calls the present into question or promises a way out of it. Thus the fulsome claim of the present arrangement is premised on hopelessness. This insidious form of realized eschatology requires persons to live without

hope. The present is unending in its projection, un-compromising in its claim of loyalty, and unac-commodating in having its own way.... I believe the Solomonic regime created such a situation of des-pair. Inevitably it had to hold on desperately and despairingly to the present, for if the present slipped away, there would be nothing. The future had al-ready been annulled. (60)

Validating an evolving and future reality must be a part of the prophet's call to live genuinely. The acceptance of the inherited sin in *The House of the Seven Gables* perpetuates this sense of a future-less existence. But in her first brave steps toward opening the cent shop in order to provide for her brother's future, Hepzibah initiates a break from the "royal consciousness" that kept her locked in the static—and as such hopeless—category of fine lady. Her struggle to step out of the numbing status quo contrasts with Uncle Venner's easy relationship with past, present, and future. But his ex-ample foreshadows the liberation that Hepzibah and her cir-cle will ultimately achieve.

The restorations that come about in *The House of the Seven Gables* and *The Scarlet Letter* exhibit the positive devel-opment that can come from constructive relationships with temporality and an understanding of grief lodged in a com-passionate heart. But "The Gentle Boy" and "The Minister's Black Veil" present more challenging explorations of prophe-cy in that they do not offer endings of satisfying restoration. To be sure, positive transformation takes place in both sto-ries. In "The Gentle Boy," legislation that bans the abuse of Quakers is instigated, and the animosity between the Quak-ers and Puritans in the town softens over the years. "The

Minister's Black Veil" offers less closure: the only essential developments, which cannot decisively be termed positive, lie in the hearts and minds of those who become Hooper's devotees. Their ability to dwell in proximity to the mystery of the veil prompts their transformation. Hawthorne makes it difficult to put a finger on the nature of this transformation. The devotees, among them Hooper's onetime fiancée, do not appear happier than the other townspeople, but they do appear less frustrated. They have moved beyond any superficial desire to remove the veil. Slight though this growth may seem, it reflects a stance that Hawthorne takes seriously: an acceptance of the unknowableness of the divine relationship with humanity. Citing Walter Benjamin, Michael Fishbane asserts that "truth is not 'an unveiling which destroys the secret, but the revelation which does it justice'" (Fishbane, 45). In creating an uncomfortable narrative in which mystery can change hearts because of its utter impenetrability, Hawthorne does justice to that mystery.

Søren Kierkegaard explores this manner of religious mystery in his writings on Christianity. Hooper's veil suggests mystery that may not be limited to a Christian response, but Kirekegaard's words advance the kind of attitude toward mystery that "The Minister's Black Veil" encourages:

> Suppose that Christianity was and wants to be a mystery, an utter mystery, not a theatrical mystery that is revealed in the fifth act, although the clever spectator already sees through it in the course of the exposition…Suppose that it does not want to be understood and that the maximum of any eventual understanding is to understand that it cannot be

understood… Suppose that speculating is a temptation, the most precarious of all. (214)

Those in Hooper's community who engage in speculation
about the veil are not bad people. Most of them are thoughtful and sincere, and readers may identify more closely with
these observers than with the devotees who are mysterious in
their own way. The attainment of a consciousness driven by
an understanding that "speculating is a temptation, the most
precarious of all" is reached by an ascetic few.

Might Hester Prynne stand among those few? She certainly realizes that publicly questioning her punishment
would not better the communal opinion of her. She also
knows that in praying for her enemies, her prayers might
somehow twist into curses, so she resists doing this as well.
But where she shows her understanding of the precarious-
ness of speculation is in her aversion to her sense of the sins
of others. She would prefer to maintain that those who do
not admit sin have not engaged in sinful acts. Perhaps this is
connected to the secrets she holds in her own heart that she
intends or has promised to withhold from the community.
Ultimately, indulging in speculation would hinder her prophetic abilities to heal her community and their response to
her. If the suffering servant devotes energy to questioning the
motivation behind the actions of the townspeople, she may
swiftly lose her ability to triumph over those actions with
compassion.

But speculating on the nature of humanity is different
from speculating on the nature of the divine. While human
beings are infinitely complex, Hawthorne's prophet stories
would suggest that God is infinitely mysterious. "The Minister's Black Veil" shows the darker side of that mystery, but

other works, such as *The House of the Seven Gables*, show the growth that can come from yielding to mystery. When the protagonists enter the thresholds of experience through which they operate out of a prophetic perfect reality, they fling themselves open to uncertainty. Hepzibah responds to uncertainty by striving to assert faith in God amid hopelessness. Her expressions of faith seem to stem from her compassion for her brother, as her prayers seek his protection. Clifford grows when he is able to give himself over to a new vision for the future, and as he asserts a faith in the vision of an upwardly migrating humanity, he gains youthful vitality and release from the weights of a past that had all but crippled him.

Perhaps if Catharine of "The Gentle Boy" could have espoused a prophetic vision that grew out of memories of a fruitful, positive past, as well as out of her experience of grief, she might have been able to envision a future that inspired her audience, not merely alarmed them. Still, Catharine's utterance stands firmly in the biblical prophetic tradition of woe oracles that are meant to spur an audience out of complacency and into action. Her isolation from the community she seeks to change also reflects that tradition. However, in Hawthorne's tale, the separation between the prophet and her audience, or perhaps even more the lack of compassion each has for the other, stunts the potential for the growth of both parties. Those best able to nurture, or to commit to a positive vision in the face of uncertainty, seem best able to live productively themselves.

Yet to what degree is the prophet's aim to live productively? If we turn to the quintessential biblical description of assessing a prophet's effectiveness in Deuteronomy 18:18–

22, the challenging answer seems to be that prophets are effective if their prophecies come to pass:

> I will raise them up a Prophet from among their brethren, like unto thee, and will put my words in his mouth; and he shall speak unto them all that I shall command him. And it shall come to pass, that whosoever will not hearken unto my words which he shall speak in my name, I will require it of him. But the prophet, which shall presume to speak a word in my name, which I have not commanded him to speak, or that shall speak in the name of other gods, even that prophet shall die. And if thou say in thine heart, How shall we know the word which the LORD hath not spoken? When a prophet speaketh in the name of the LORD, if the thing follow not, nor come to pass, that is the thing which the LORD hath not spoken, but the prophet hath spoken it presumptuously: thou shalt not be afraid of him.

This last verse is cautiously phrased: if the prophecy does not come to pass, then it did not come from God. But if the prophet speaks it "presumptuously," or out of pride, the people need not fear him. He is not necessarily evil or even false. He need not be banished or even killed; he simply need not be feared. We may seldom know if a prophet is "genuine." There is no timeframe laid out within which the prophecy must come to pass. If there is an infinite amount of time for the prophecy to be realized, then the standards by which we judge prophetic words lie beyond what humanity can measure. Or it may be that the open-ended nature of the "true" prophetic utterance leaves us with a realization that we should not attempt to judge it at all.

And Hawthorne's narratives are so constructed that they, like the prophetic language they contain, resist a final analysis. This is what gives them their quality of constituting an American mythology that simultaneously questions American mythology. As Broek remarks,

> This sense of one's perceptions as always contingent and liable to cancellation or revision by a stronger "Other" is at the heart of the conflicts illuminated by Hawthorne and Melville. As Coverdale cannot "see" the Veiled Lady, as Bartleby goes blind, as Hepzibah squints and as the "A" is a symbol that resists transformation..., what is revealed is the "truth" that no story, symbol system, or faith is ever entire or sufficient. (Broek, 13)

It is imperative that we never know what's behind the veil, can never pin down a final, authoritative meaning for Hester's *A*. The inherent good in these stories is found in those who move away from stasis and—through compassion— toward a world whose margin fades forever and forever when they move.

For if there are as many types of prophecies as there are prophets, then assessing the quality or validity of the prophecy is a near impossible task. Aviva Zornberg cites the Talmudic saying that "'Two prophets do not prophesy in the same style.' The true prophet has a unique voice; he conveys what he has heard, according to his own strength, as fully as he can bear it" (277). The variety of prophetic voices in Hawthorne's fiction attests to this reality. At some level, they all reach toward Hawthorne's own sense of the importance of seeking new ways to live religiously: "We certainly do need a new revelation—a new system—for there seems to be no life in the old one" (*The American Notebooks*, 352). The work of Hawthorne's prophets does not guarantee the success of or even necessarily establish a "new system." But the sincerity with which they engage in their prophetic work, in which they convey what they know as fully as they can bear it, establishes the literary foundation of a nation. Hawthorne was painfully aware of the troubled and tenuous origins of America. Yet if English national mythology was viewed with authority and reverence, he asserted that his nation also had a mythology of national origin. For Hawthorne, American literature, shaped by a mysterious, nuanced past, holds space for hope in the brave and tender hearts of her prophets.

Bibliography

Abbott, Marjorie Post, et al. Historical Dictionary of the Friends (Quakers). Scarecrow Press, 2003.

Albanese, Catherine L. America: Religions and Religion. 4th ed. Wadsworth, 2007.

Allen, Leslie C. Jeremiah: A Commentary. Westminster John Knox, 2008.

Bacher, Wilhelm and Jacob Zallel Lauterbach. "Parable." Jewish Encyclopedia.com. Web. 1 March 2010. https://jewishencyclopedia.com/articles/10459-mashal.

Battaglia, Francis Joseph. "The House of the Seven Gables: New Light on Old Problems." PMLA 82 (1967): 579–590.

Becker, John E. Hawthorne's Historical Allegory: An Examination of the American Conscience. Kennikat, 1971.

Beegle, Dewey M. "Moses." The Anchor Bible Dictionary, vol. 4. Ed. David Noel Freedman. Doubleday, 1992.

Bell, Millicent. Hawthorne's View of the Artist. State University of New York Press, 1962.

Bercovitch, Sacvan. The American Jeremiad. The University of Wisconsin Press, 1978.

———. The Puritan Origins of the American Self. Yale University Press, 1975.

———. The Office of the Scarlet Letter. Johns Hopkins University Press, 1991.

Blenkinsopp, Joseph. Isaiah 1-39: A New Translation with Introduction and Commentary. Doubleday, 2000.

Bloom, Harold, editor. Hester Prynne. Chelsea House Publishers, 1990.

Bowker, J. W. "Prophetic Action and Sacramental Form." *Studia Ev angelica* 3 (1964).

Broek, Michael. "Were It a New-Made World: Hawthorne, Melville, and the Unmasking of America." *European Journal of American Studies*, vol. 5, no. 1 (2010): 1–16.

Brueggemann, Walter. *The Prophetic Imagination*. 2nd ed. Augsburg Fortress, 2011.

Childs, Brevard S. *The Book of Exodus: A Critical, Theological Commentary*. The Westminster Press, 1974.

Coale, Samuel Chase. *Mesmerism and Hawthorne: Mediums of American Romance*. University of Alabama Press, 1998.

Cochran, Robert W. "Hawthorne's Choice: The Veil or the Jaundiced Eye." *College English* 23 (1962): 342–346.

Colacurcio, Michael J. *The Province of Piety: Moral History in Hawthorne's Early Tales*. Harvard University Press, 1984.

Crews, Frederick. *The Sins of the Fathers: Hawthorne's Psychological Themes*. Oxford University Press, 1966.

Crowley, J. Donald, ed. *Hawthorne: The Critical Heritage*. Routledge, 1970.

Davis, Clark. *Hawthorne's Shyness: Ethics, Politics, and the Question of Engagement*. Johns Hopkins University Press, 2005.

Davitt Bell, Michael. *Hawthorne and the Historical Romance of New England*. Princeton University Press, 1971.

De Vries, Simon. *From Old Revelation to New: A Tradition-Historical and Redaction-Critical Study of Temporal Transitions in Prophetic Prediction*. Eerdmans Publishing Company, 1995.

Dodd, Charles Harold. *The Parables of the Kingdom*. 1935. Scribner, 1961.

Donohue, Agnes McNeill. *Hawthorne: Calvin's Ironic Stepchild*. Kent State University Press, 1985.

Doubleday, Neal Frank. *Hawthorne's Early Tales: A Critical Study*. Duke University Press, 1972.

Duguid, Iain M. "Did a Prophet Really Lay on His Side for More than a Year? (Ezekiel 4)." *Crossway*, 12 November 2022, https://www.crossway.org/articles/did-a-lprophet-really-lay-on-his-side-for-more-than-a-year-ezekiel-4/.

Ellwood, Gracia Fay. Message to the author. 10 January. 2010, email.

Fishbane, Michael. *The Garments of Torah: Essays in Biblical Hermeneutics*. Indiana University Press, 1989.

Fogle, Richard Harter. *Hawthorne's Fiction: The Light & the Dark*. 1st ed.University of Oklahoma Press, 1952.

Fox, George. *Journal of George Fox*. Edited by J. L. Nickalls. Cambridge University Press, 1952.

Friebel, Kelvin. "A Hermeneutical Paradigm for Interpreting Prophetic Sign-Actions."*Didaskalia* 12 (2001): 25–45.

Folsom, James K. *Man's Accidents and God's Purposes: Multiplicity in Hawthorne's Fiction*. College and UP, 1963.

Gatta, Jr., John. "Progress and Providence in *The House of the Seven Gables*." *American Literature* 50 (1978): 37–48.

Gable, Harvey L. *Liquid Fire: Transcendental Mysticism in the Romances of Nathaniel Hawthorne*. P. Lang, 1998.

Gollin, Rita K., John L. Idol, and Sterling K. Eisiminger, eds. *Prophetic Pictures: Nathaniel Hawthorne's Knowledge and Uses of the Visual Arts*. Greenwood Press, 1991.

Hals, Ronald M. *Ezekiel*. William B. Eerdmans Publishing Company, 1989.

Hawthorne, Nathaniel. *Hawthorne as Editor: Selections from His Writings in the American Magazine of Useful and Entertaining Knowledge*. Edited by Arlin Turner. Louisiana State University Press, 1941.

———. *Mosses from an Old Manse*. Edited by William Charvat, et al. Ohio State University Press, 1974.

———. *The American Notebooks*. Edited by Claude M. Simpson, et al. Ohio State University Press, 1972.

———. *The Blithedale Romance and Fanshawe*. Edited by Claude M. Simpson, et al. Ohio State University Press, 1971.

———. *The House of the Seven Gables*. Edited by William Charvat, et al. Ohio State University Press, 1974.

———. *The Scarlet Letter*. Edited by William Charvat, et al. Ohio State University Press, 1962.

————. *The Snow-Image and Uncollected Tales.* Edited by William Charvat, et al. Ohio State University Press, 1974.

————. *Twice Told Tales.* Edited by William Charvat, et al. Columbus: Ohio State University Press, 1965.

Hedrick, Charles W. "Parable." *The New Interpreter's Dictionary of the Bible.* Edited by Katharine Doob Sakenfeld, et al. Vol. 4. Abingdon Press, 2009.

Heschel, Abraham J. *The Prophets.* Harper and Row, 1962.

Honing, Edwin. *Dark Conceit: The Making of Allegory.* Northwestern University Press, 1959.

Hudspeth, Robert. Message to the author. 30 September. 2009, email.

James, Henry. *Hawthorne.* Harper & Brothers, 1880.

Jemielity, Thomas. *Satire and the Hebrew Prophets.* Westminster/John Knox Press, 1992.

Kierkegaard, Søren. *Concluding Unscientific Postscript to* Philosophical Fragments. Edited and translated by Howard V. Hong and Edna H. Hong. Vol. 1. Princeton University Press, 1992.

Jones, Lindsay, et al., editors. *Encyclopedia of Religion.* 2nd ed. Vol. 10. Thompson Gale, 2005.

Keil, Carl Friedrich and Franz Delitzsch. *Biblical Commentary on the Old Testament.* 1876. Translated by Geoffrey R. Bromiley. Eerdmans, 1949.

Knierim, Rolf. "Criticism of Literary Features, Form, Tradition, and Redaction." *The Hebrew Bible and Its Modern Interpreters.* Edited by Douglas A. Knight and Gene M. Tucker. Fortress Press, 1985.

Landy, Francis. *Hosea.* Sheffield Academic Press, 1995.

Lang, Bernhard. "Street Theater, Raising the Dead, and the Zoroastrian Connection in Ezekiel's Prophecy." *Ezekiel and His Book.* Edited by J. Lust, et al. Leuven University Press, 1986. 297–316.

Lang, Bernhard. *Monotheism and the Prophetic Minority: An Essay in Biblical History and Sociology.* Almond Press, 1983.

Levin, Harry. *The Power of Blackness: Hawthorne, Poe, Melville.* Knopf, 1958.

Loges, Max. "Hawthorne's *The House of the Seven Gables.*" *Explicator* 60 (2002): 64–66.

Lundbom, Jack R. *Jeremiah 21-36: A New Translation with Introduction and Commentary.* The Anchor Bible/Doubleday, 2004.

Masui, Shitsuyo. "Reading Hawthorne in the Context of The American Popular Religion." Diss. Boston University, 1996.

Matthews, Victor H. "Cloth, Clothes." *The New Interpreter's Dictionary of the Bible.* Edited by Katharine Doob Sakenfeld, et al. Vol. 1. Abingdon Press, 2006.

Matthiessen, Francis Otto. *American Renaissance: Art and Expression in the Age of Emerson and Whitman.* Oxford University Press, 1941.

McCarthy, Judy. "'The Minister's Black Veil': Concealing Moses and the Holy of Holies." *Studies in Short Fiction* 24 (1987): 131–138.

McPherson, Hugo. *Hawthorne as Myth-Maker: A Study in Imagination.* University of Toronto Press, 1969.

McWilliams, Wilson Carey. *The Idea of Fraternity in America.* University of California Press, 1973.

Montgomery, Marion. *Why Hawthorne was Melancholy.* 1st ed. Sherwood Sugden, 1984.

Moore, Margaret B. *The Salem World of Nathaniel Hawthorne.* University of Missouri Press, 1998.]

Olson, Dennis T. "Moses." *The New Interpreter's Dictionary of the Bible.* Edited by Katharine Doob Sakenfeld, et al. Vol. 4. Abingdon Press, 2006.

Orians, G. Harrison. "The Sources and Themes of Hawthorne's 'The Gentle Boy.'" *New England Quarterly: A Historical Review of New England Life and Letters* 14 (1941): 664–678.

The Nathaniel Hawthorne Journal. NCR Microcard Editions, 1971.

Newberry, Frederick. "The Biblical Veil: Sources and Typology in Hawthorne's 'The Minister's Black Veil.'" *Texas Studies in Literature and Language* 32 (1989): 169–195.

Perrin, Norman. *What is Redaction Criticism?* Fortress Press, 1969.

Propp, William H. C. *Exodus 19-40: A New Translation with Introduction and Commentary.* The Anchor Bible/Doubleday, 2006.

Reynolds, Larry J. *Devils and Rebels: The Making of Hawthorne's Damned Politics.* University of Michigan Press, 2008.

Rice, Julian C. "The Unimpaled Butterfly: Redemption in The House of the Seven Gables." *Journal of Evolutionary Psychology* 2 (August 1981): 48-62.

Shulman, George. *American Prophecy: Race and Redemption in American Political Culture.* University of Minnesota Press, 2008.

Spiller, Robert. "The Mind and Art of Nathaniel Hawthorne." *The Outlook* 149 (1928): 650-652; 676; 678.

Stacey, W. David. *Prophetic Drama in the Old Testament.* Epworth Press, 1990.

Stein, William Bysshe. *Hawthorne's Faust: A Study of the Devil Archetype.* University of Florida Press, 1953.

Sternberg, Meir. *The Poetics of Biblical Narrative: Ideological Literature and the Drama of Reading.* Indiana University Press, 1987.

Stewart, Randall. *Nathaniel Hawthorne: a Biography.* Yale University Press, 1948.

Studies in Puritan American Spirituality. Edwin Mellen Press, 1990.

Sweeney, Marvin A. *I & II Kings: A Commentary.* Westminster John Knox Press, 2007.

———. "Isaiah 1-4 and the Post-Exilic Understanding of the Isaianic Tradition." Diss. Claremont Graduate University, 1983.

———. *Isaiah 1-39: With an Introduction to Prophetic Literature.* William B. Eerdmans Publishing Company, 1996.

———. Message to the author. 8 May 2007. email.

———. Message to the author. 6 August. 2009. email.

———. Message to the author. 10 December. 2009. email.

———. *Reading the Hebrew Bible After the Shoah: Engaging Holocaust Theology.* Fortress Press, 2008.

————. *The Prophetic Literature*. Abingdon Press, 2006.

————. *The Twelve Prophets*, vol. 1. The Liturgical Press, 2000.

Tharpe, Jac. *Nathaniel Hawthorne: Identity and Knowledge*. Southern Illinois University Press, 1967.

Thompson, W. R. "Patterns of Biblical Allusions in Hawthorne's 'The Gentle Boy.'" *South Central Bulletin* 22 (1962): 3–10.

Tocqueville, Alexis de. *Democracy in America*. Trans Harvey C. Mansfield and Delba Winthrop. Chicago: University of Chicago Press, 2000.

Turner, Arlin. *Nathaniel Hawthorne: A Biography*. Oxford University Press, 1980.

Via, Dan Otto, Jr. *The Parables: Their Literary and Existential Dimension*. Fortress Press, 1967.

Voight, Gilbert P. "The Meaning of 'The Minister's Black Veil.'" *College English* 13 (1952): 337–338.

Westermann, Claus. *Basic Forms of Prophetic Speech*. Trans Hugh Clayton White. The Westminster Press, 1967.

Wheeler, Otis B. "Love Among the Ruins: Hawthorne's Surrogate Religion." *The Southern Review* 10 (1974): 535–65.

Wildberger, Hans. *Isaiah: A Continental Commentary*. Translated by Thomas H. Trapp. Fortress Press, 1991.

Winthrop, John. "A Model of Christian Charity." *Puritans in the New World: A Critical Anthology*, edited by David Hall. Princeton University Press, 2004.

Yee, Gale A. *Composition and Tradition in the Book of Hosea: A Redaction Critical Investigation*. Scholars Press, 1987.

INDEX

Stories and Characters

Biblical References